Table of Contents

Table of Contents

Frank Schaffer Publications®

Send all inquiries to:
Frank Schaffer Publications
3195 Wilson Drive NW
Grand Rapids, Michigan 49534

Science—Grade 6

ISBN 0-7696-4946-7

1 2 3 4 5 6 7 8 9 10 WAL 10 09 08 07 06

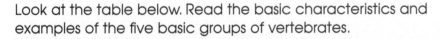

The animal kingdom is divided into two main groups—invertebrates and vertebrates. An invertebrate is an animal without a backbone. A vertebrate is an animal with a backbone. Only 4 percent of the approximately 1.5 million known species on Earth are vertebrates. Vertebrates can be divided into five categories, or types. The types are fish, amphibians, reptiles, birds, and mammals. Of the 4 percent of known species that are vertebrates, only a small fraction are mammals.

Look at the table below. Read the basic characteristics and examples of the five basic groups of vertebrates.

GROUP	CHARACTERISTICS	EXAMPLES
Fish	Most often a cold-blooded water creature with an elongated body and fins and gills	Sharks and bony fish such as trout, bass, and tuna
Amphibians	Most often a cold-blooded creature with young that live in the water and use gills to breathe and adults that are air-breathing	Frogs, toads, and salamanders
Reptiles	Most often an animal that crawls or moves on the ground on its belly; has a bony skeleton and is covered with scales or bony plates	Snakes, lizards, alligators, and turtles
Birds	Most often a warm-blooded animal that is covered with feathers, has hollow bones, and has forelimbs modified into wings	Robins, ostriches, ducks, and geese
Mammals	Most often a warm-blooded animal that feeds its young with milk; has skin and is often covered with hair; gives birth to live young	Humans, dogs, whales, platypuses, bats, and apes

While vertebrates are different in many ways, as shown in the table, they also have significant similarities. All of the animals use food to obtain and maintain energy. They all reproduce, give off waste products, and respond to the environment. Vertebrates also are bilaterally symmetrical. This means that the left and right sides of the body are alike. More advanced vertebrates have necks, while others are usually divided into a head and trunk.

Types of vertebrates are found throughout the world. Certain species are able to survive the polar freeze. Others can live in the tropics. All of these animals have responded to their environment by utilizing the world around them, using available food, water, and shelter. Often, animals will change over hundreds of years to adapt to changes that occur in their natural habitat; for example, growing a thicker or thinner coat of fur as a body covering.

Invertebrates are also found throughout the world. They are varied in characteristics. The invertebrates are often categorized into eight different groups. The following chart shows the different types, the characteristics, and examples of each.

GROUP	CHARACTERISTICS	EXAMPLES
Sponges	Vary in shape and size depending on environment; adult sponges live attached to items in the water and never move; they reproduce sexually and asexually	Sponges
Cnidarians	Hollow-bodied organisms with stinging cells; many have snake-like tentacles that capture food and help them move	Coral, jellyfish, and sea anemones
Flatworms	The simplest type of worm; most are parasites; others live in fresh- or saltwater	Tapeworms and flukes
Roundworms	Found almost everywhere in the world; most are free-living in the soil; more complex than the flatworm; a parasite	Nematodes and hookworms
Annelids	Most are free-living and live in the soils; some, such as leeches, are parasitic; complex enough to have systems for circulating blood, sensing stimuli, reproduction, and movement	Earthworms and leeches
Mollusks	Soft bodies generally, but not always; covered with a hard shell; has a special fold of skin called the *mantle*; a foot aids in movement and capturing prey	Clams, squid, and snails
Echinoderms	Live in oceans and are covered in spines, which are actually bony plates of the skeleton	Sea stars and sand dollars
Arthropods	1 million known species of arthropods on earth; external skeletons, jointed legs	Insects, crabs, and crayfish

Name

Remember that invertebrates are animals that have no backbone. Learn about them by completing a concept map of invertebrates.

Directions: To complete the map, write one of the subgroups from the box in an empty oval. Then, branch off of each subgroup and write group names. An example is done for you. You may want to include sketches.

WORD BANK

| sponges | cnidarians | mollusks | segmented worms |
| flatworms | arthropods | roundworms | echinoderms |

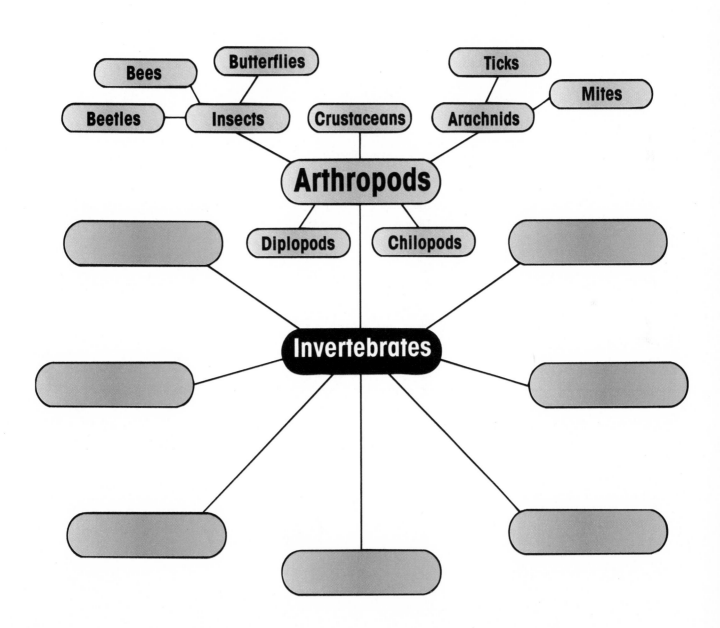

Name _____

The largest percentage of animals in the world are arthropods. Arthropods are animals with exoskeletons and jointed appendages. They live in all parts of the world and in every type of habitat.

Directions: Look at the list of arthropods below. Print the names of insects in the square, the names of arachnids in the triangle, and the names of crustaceans in the circle.

WORD BANK

tarantula	bee	mite	crab
lobster	butterfly	scorpion	wasp
beetle	shrimp	hornet	fly
grasshopper	cricket	crayfish	tick
garden spider	brown recluse	black widow	cicada
barnacle	louse	water flea	aphid
termite	ant	wood louse	flea
moth	firefly	gnat	mayfly

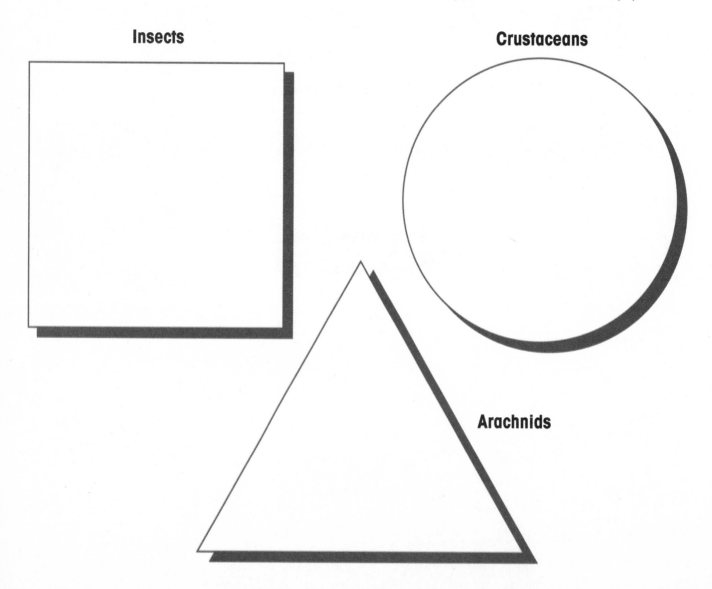

Insects

Crustaceans

Arachnids

Name

The oceans are teeming with living things.

Directions: Complete the word grid below to learn the names of some marine life.

WORD BANK

conch	eel	lobster	octopus	shrimp	starfish
coral	hermit crab	manatee	scallop	sponge	triton
dolphin	limpet	mussel	seal	squid	whale

M A R I N E L I F E

Name _____

Directions: Circle the correct answers.

1. Natural selection is the process by which organisms that are best suited for their environment are successful in living and reproducing.

   true or false

2. One adaptation animals have made to hide by blending in with their surroundings is called

   a. sense of smell.

   b. camouflage.

   c. eating more.

3. Many animals have ways to defend themselves. Which of the following is NOT a way they protect themselves?

   a. hiding

   b. color

   c. senses

   d. spray/taste

   e. food

Directions: Answer the following using complete sentences.

1. What are some ways wildlife use their environment to live and survive?

   _____

   _____

2. Compare and contrast how humans and animals make use of their environment for survival. Use the Venn diagram.

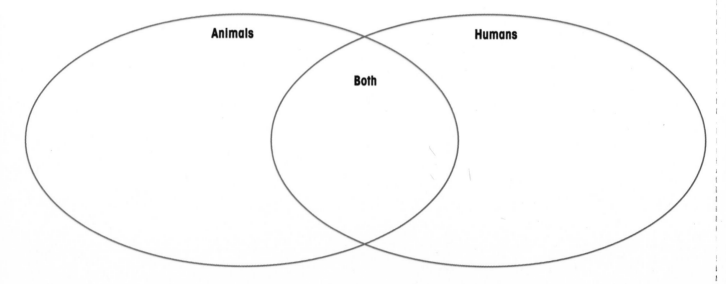

Animals   Humans

Both

Metamorphosis

Certain animals go through big physical changes as part of their development. There are two kinds of change: an incomplete metamorphosis and a complete metamorphosis. A **complete metamorphosis** means the organism goes through four stages of growth and can look very different from the adult organism. An **incomplete metamorphosis** means the change in the organism is not complete—meaning the young may resemble the adult.

Directions: Look at the cycles below. Label the stages of complete and incomplete metamorphosis. Use the words from the WORD BANK.

WORD BANK

complete	adult	larva	nymph
incomplete	egg	pupa	

A. _____ **Metamorphosis**

4. _____

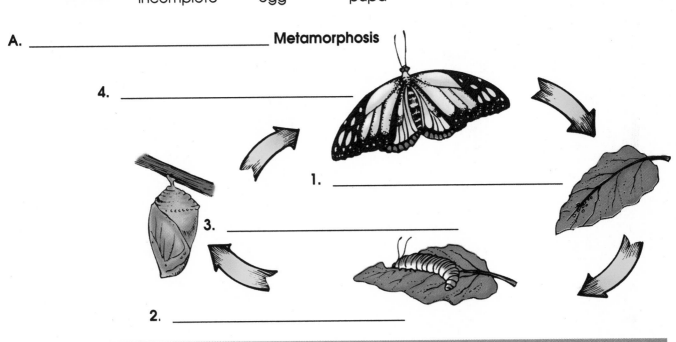

1. _____

3. _____

2. _____

B. _____ **Metamorphosis**

3. _____

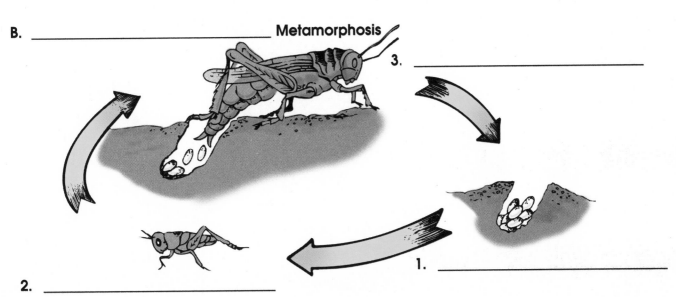

1. _____

2. _____

 Science: Grade 6

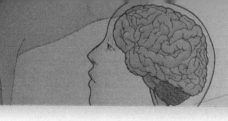

Name _____

Your body is made of many systems which work together. These systems work in groups.

Directions: Use the words from the WORD BANK to label the different body systems in each group.

 WORD BANK

skeletal	muscular	digestive
respiratory	circulatory	urinary
nervous	sensory	endocrine

MOVEMENT GROUP

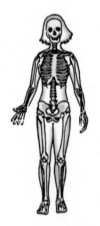 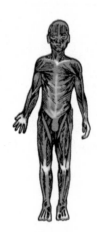

CONTROL GROUP

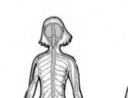 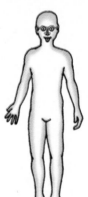 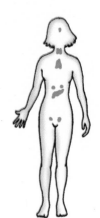

_____ _____   _____ _____ _____

ENERGY GROUP

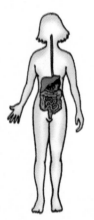 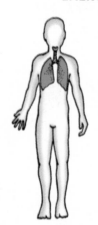  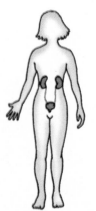

_____ _____   _____   _____

10 *Science: Grade 6*

Name _____

Directions: Label the bones of the hand and foot.

 WORD BANK   **Common Name (*Scientific Name*)**

digits (*phalanges*)   instep (*metatarsals*)
wrist (*carpals*)   digits (*phalanges*)
ankle (*tarsals*)   palm (*metacarpals*)

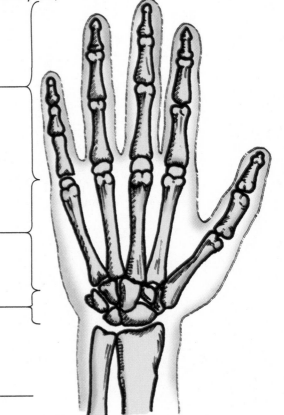

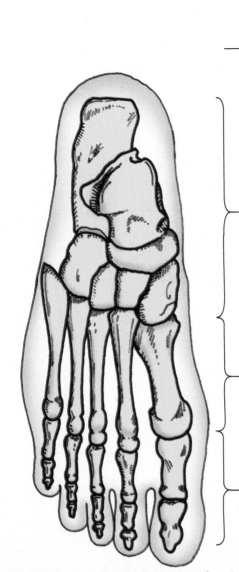

11   *Science: Grade 6*

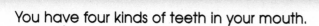

Four Kinds of Teeth

You have four kinds of teeth in your mouth.

Directions: Label the adult teeth pictured below.

WORD BANK   canines   bicuspids   incisors   molars

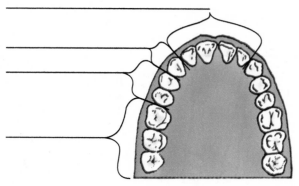

Adult upper

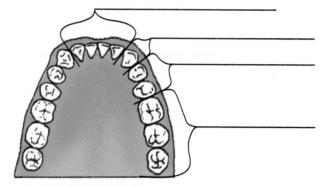

Adult lower

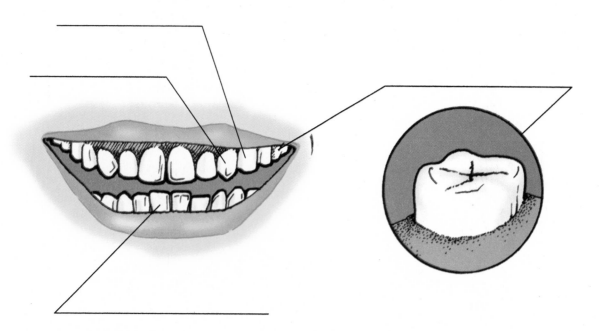

Name _____

Directions: Your teeth are made up of a number of layers. Label the layers and outside parts of the tooth below.

WORD BANK

neck	root	crown	dentin
cementum	enamel	pulp	root canal

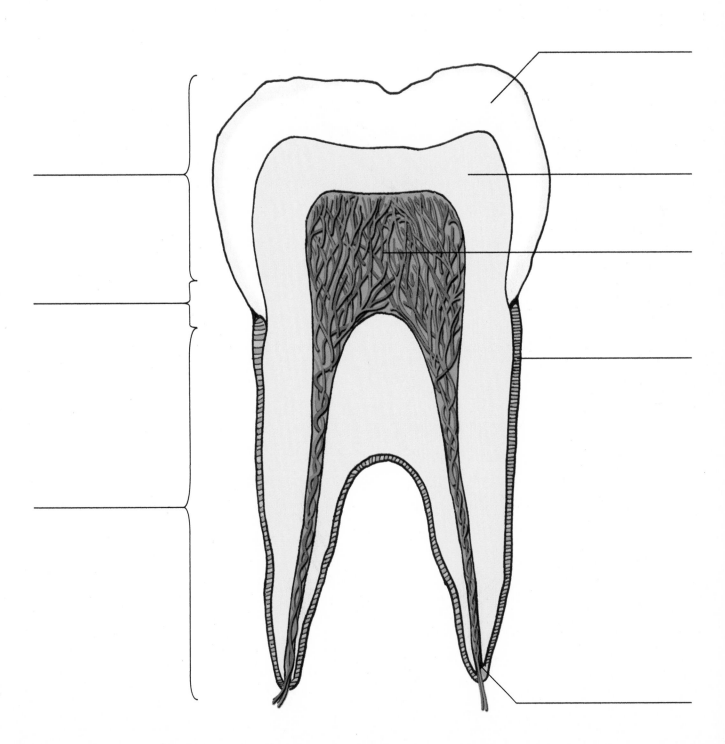

Name _____

Directions: Label the three different kinds of muscles in section **A**. Give an example of the kind of work they do. Label the muscle parts in section **B**.

WORD BANK

skeletal muscles
tendon
muscle fiber
muscle group
cardiac muscles
smooth muscles

These muscles can make your heart beat.
These muscles can move your bones.
These muscles can move food in your stomach.

A.

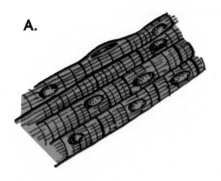 

Kind of Muscle

_____   _____   _____

Kind of Work

_____   _____   _____

Muscle Parts _____

B.

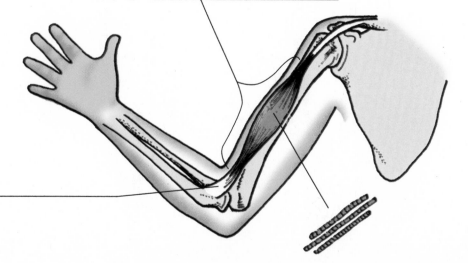

_____

Name

Skeletal muscles are attached to the skeleton by means of **tendons**.

Directions: Label the parts of the arm pictured below.

WORD BANK
tendons   shoulder blade
biceps muscle humerus
radius   ulna

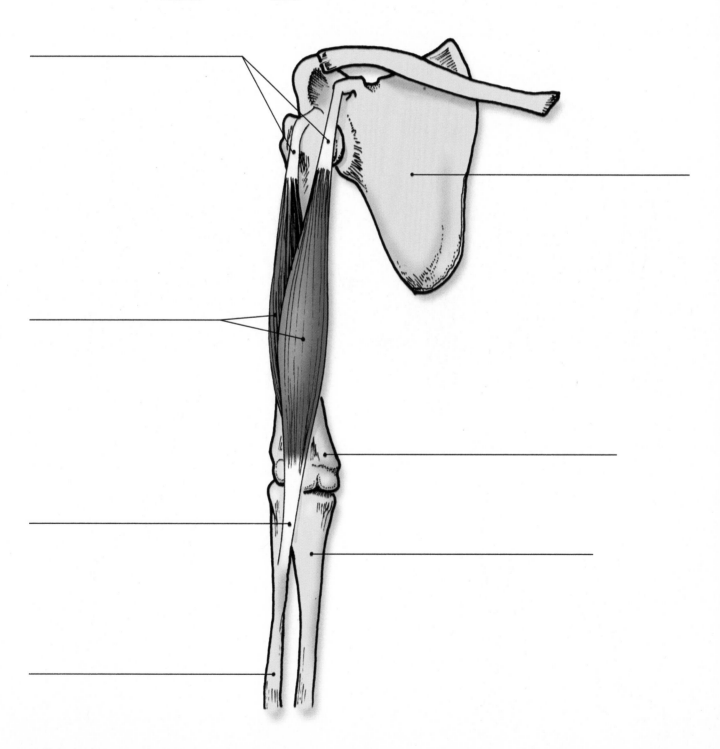

Directions: Draw red arrows on the arteries showing the flow of blood away from the heart.

Directions: Draw blue arrows on the veins showing the flow of blood back to the heart.

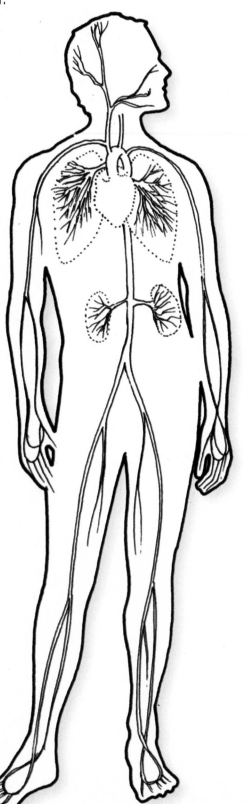

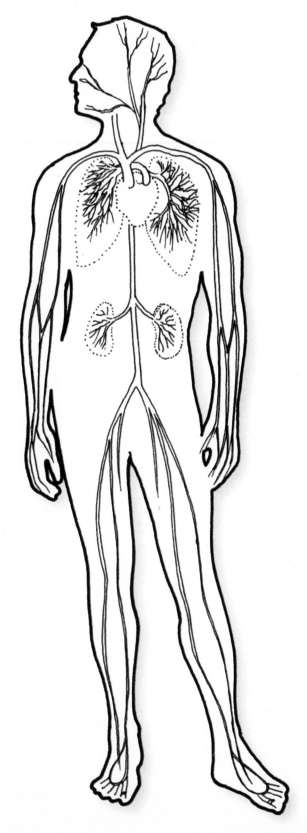

Your Heart

Directions: Label the parts of your heart.

WORD BANK

left atrium   right atrium   vena cava
left ventricle   right ventricle   aorta
pulmonary artery   pulmonary veins

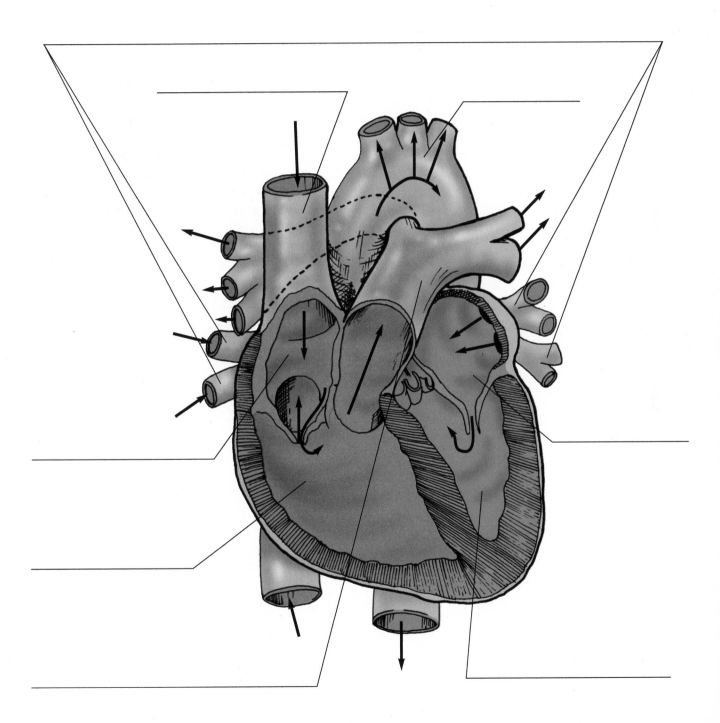

Neurons act as "go-betweens" in the sending and receiving of impulses within the nervous system. The drawings below illustrate how impulses pass from one neuron to another.

Directions: Label the parts of the enlarged illustration.

WORD BANK

synaptic cleft
axon terminal

transmitting molecule
dendrite

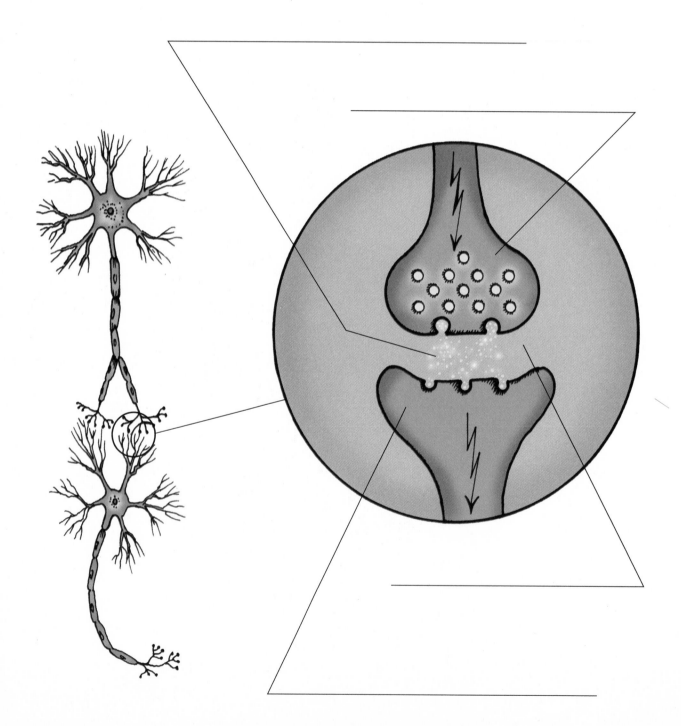

Name _____

Directions: Write the letter of each function next to its matching part.
Draw a line from the pictured part of the nervous system to its function.

PARTS

1. _____ cerebrum
2. _____ cerebellum
3. _____ medulla
4. _____ spinal cord
5. _____ spinal nerves

FUNCTION

a. It controls balance and muscular coordination.

b. It controls thought, voluntary movement, memory, and learning, and also processes information from the senses.

c. They carry impulses between the spinal cord and body parts.

d. It controls breathing, heartbeat, and other vital body processes.

e. It relays impulses between the brain and other parts of the body.

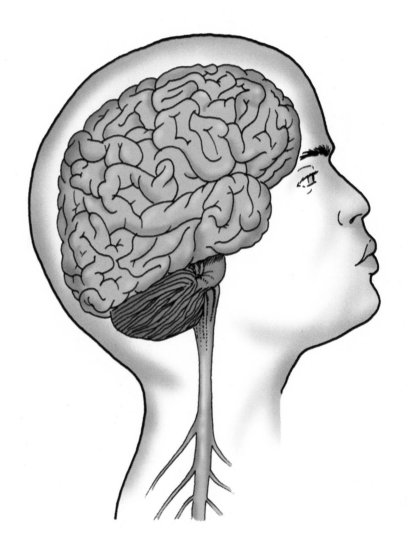

Name _____

The **autonomic nervous system** works almost independently of the central nervous system. It controls the life-sustaining functions of the body, such as breathing, digestion, and heartbeat. These organs and muscle tissues work involuntarily.

Directions: Label these important parts of the autonomic nervous system.

WORD BANK

eye	trachea	heart	lungs
liver	gallbladder	stomach	pancreas
small intestine	large intestine	rectum	

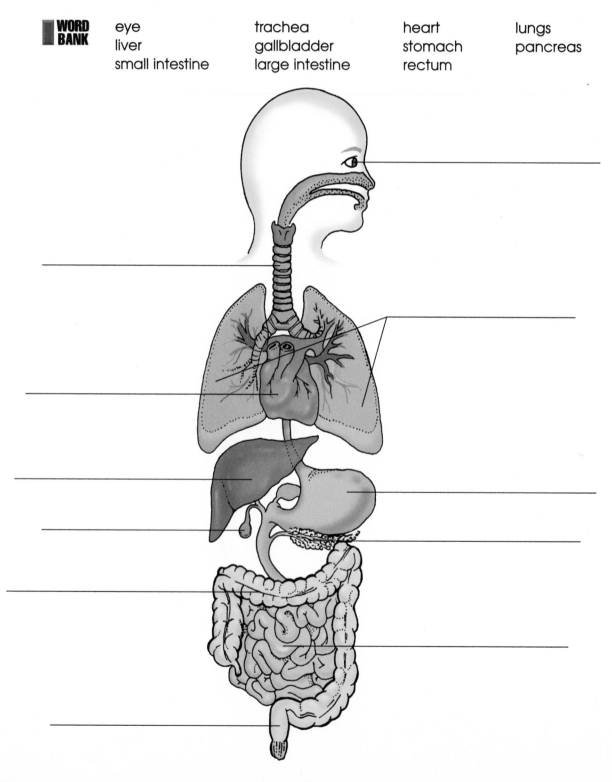

Name _____

Directions: Use the WORD BANK to complete the puzzle.

WORD BANK

cerebrum   cerebellum   brain stem   spinal cord
dendrite   axon   nucleus   neuron
medulla

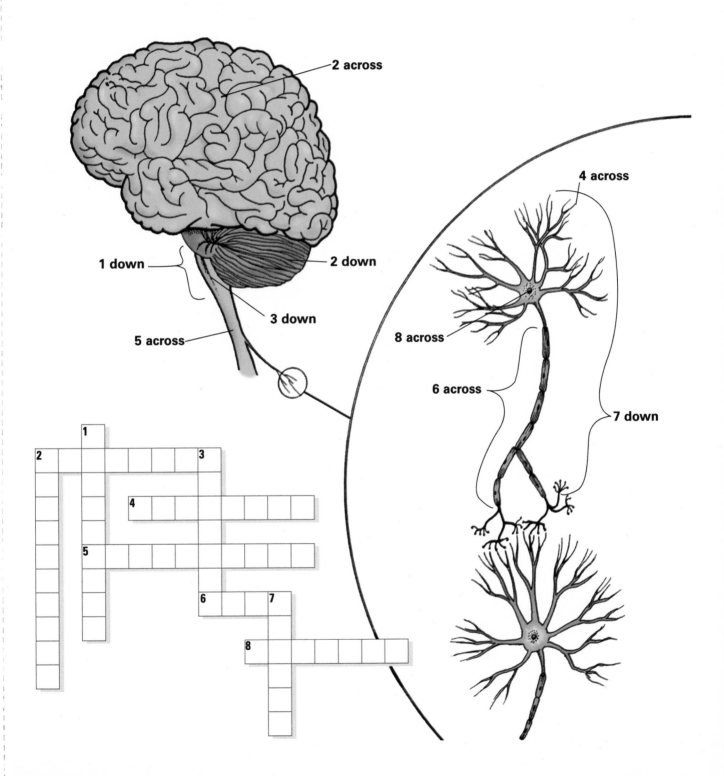

Name _____

Directions: Draw a line from the name of the gland to its picture.
Draw a line from the picture of the gland to its function.

GLAND

thyroid •

pituitary •

parathyroids •

adrenal •

thymus •

ovaries •

pancreas •

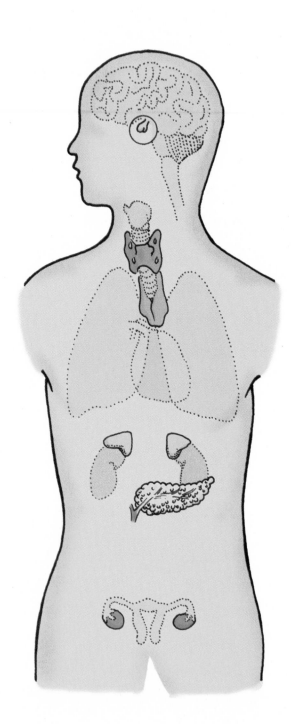

FUNCTION

• Controls other glands and body growth.

• Control the amount of calcium in your blood.

• Controls the rate that food is turned into energy.

• Helps the body's immune system to recognize and reject germs.

• Affects kidneys and helps when you are excited, angry, or frightened.

• Controls the body's use of glucose.

• Produce female characteristics and initiate female bodily functions.

Name _____

Your brain gets information from outside your body through many different sense organs.

Directions: Label the different sense organs and the nerve cell pictured on this page.

WORD BANK
eye
ear
tongue
receptor nerve cell
sensory nerve cell
nose

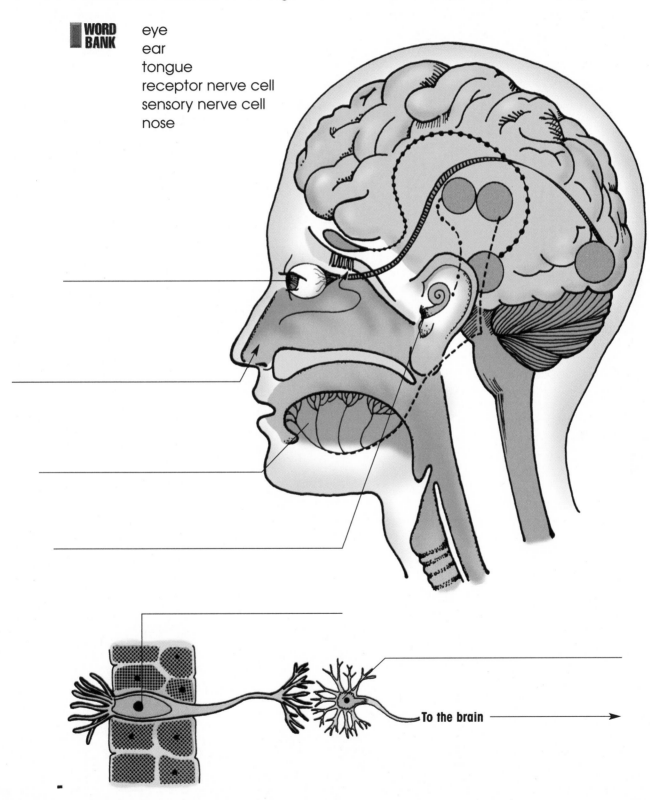

To the brain →

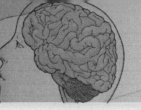

The Senses

QUESTION   What observations can I make with each of my senses?

MATERIALS   a piece of candy in a wrapper

PROCEDURE   Complete the table using your senses.

What to Do	Observations	Sense Used	Organ Used
Look at the piece of candy in the wrapper.			
Hold the candy in its wrapper.			
Hold the candy in its wrapper up to your nose.			
Listen as you open the candy wrapper.			
Hold your nose and place the candy in your mouth.			
Let go of your nose and move the candy around in your mouth.			
Listen as you move the candy around in your mouth.			
Feel the candy in your mouth.			
Look at someone else as he or she eats candy.			
Listen as he or she eats candy.			
Listen to the wrapper as you crinkle it up to throw it away.			

Directions: Answer the questions.

1. Did looking at the piece of candy help you decide what it would taste

   like? _____ Why or why not? _____

2. Which sense do you think you rely on the most? Why? _____

   _____

Name _____

Directions: Label the parts of your ear.

WORD BANK

auditory canal
hammer
stirrup
semicircular canals

auditory nerve
oval window
eardrum
anvil

cochlea
eustachian tube
wax gland
auricle

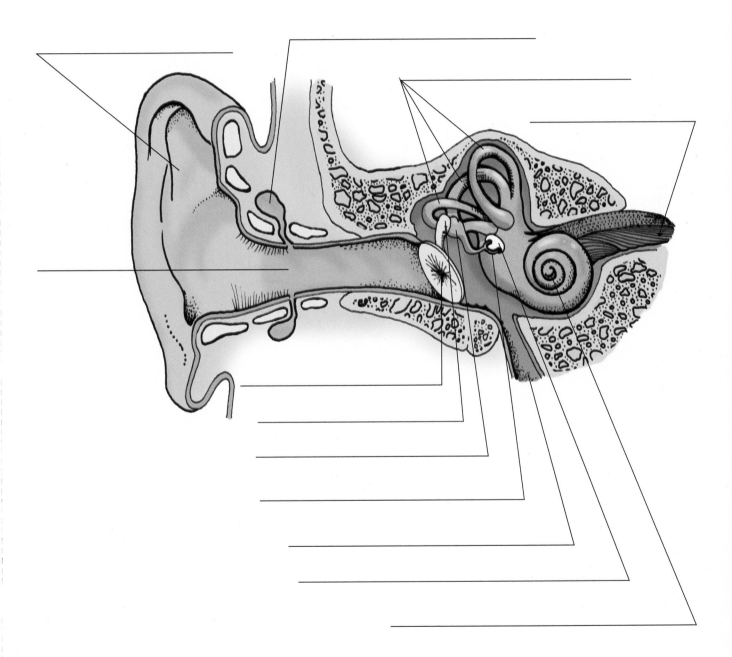

25 *Science: Grade 6*

Name _____

Directions: Label the parts of your nose.

WORD BANK   nostril   olfactory nerve   brain
                 nasal passage   receptor cells

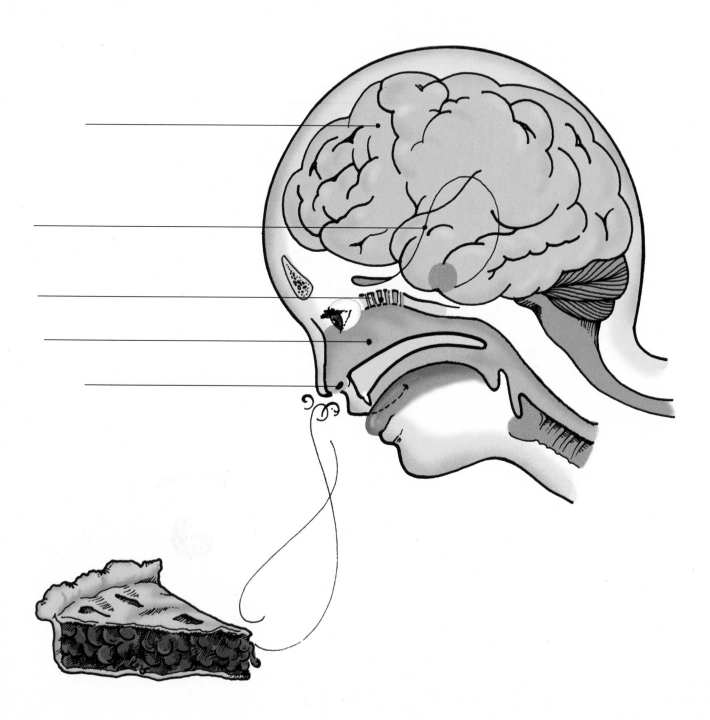

26   *Science: Grade 6*

Name

Directions: Label the parts of your eye pictured below.

WORD BANK

optic nerve   retina   lens   sclera
iris   cornea   pupil

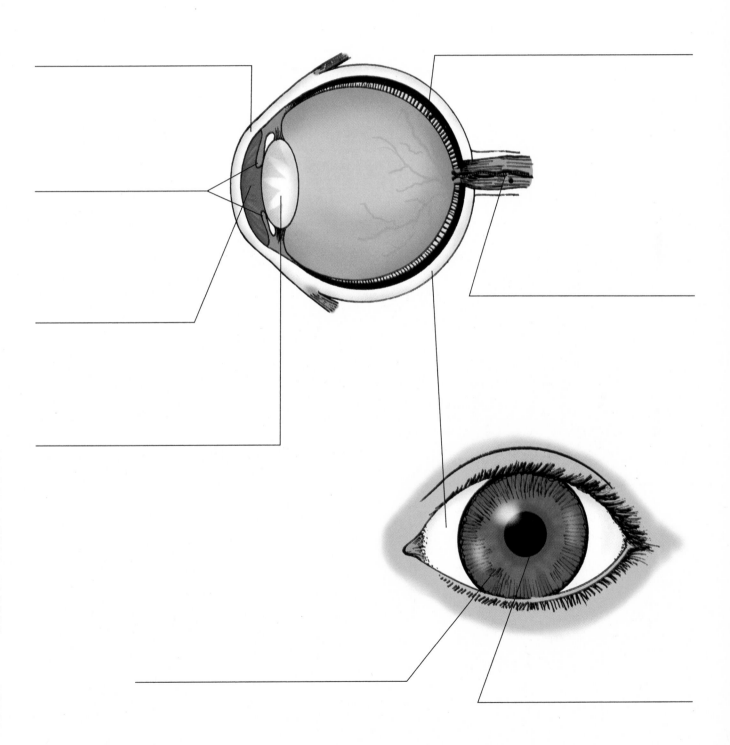

Name _____

Directions: Use the WORD BANK to complete the puzzle.

WORD BANK
- cornea
- semicircular canals
- auditory nerve
- lens
- retina
- optic nerve
- sclera
- stirrup
- cochlea
- anvil
- auricle
- eardrum
- pupil
- hammer
- iris

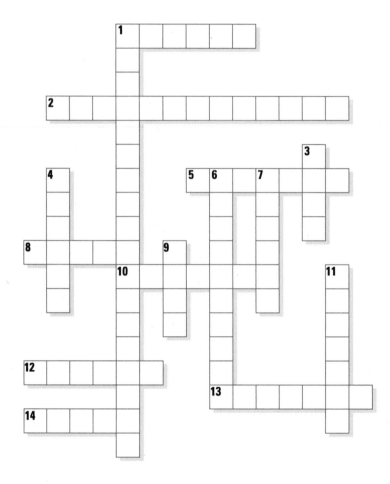

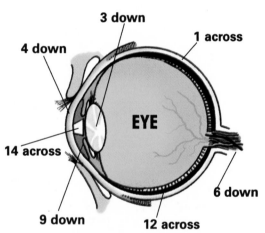

EYE

- 3 down
- 4 down
- 1 across
- 14 across
- 9 down
- 6 down
- 12 across

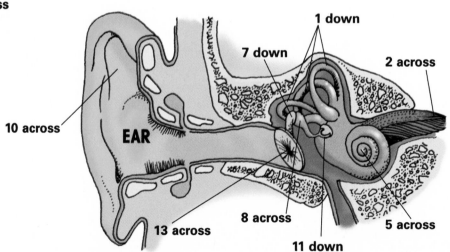

EAR

- 1 down
- 7 down
- 2 across
- 10 across
- 13 across
- 8 across
- 11 down
- 5 across

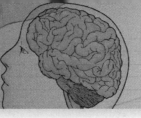

Name

Directions: Use the WORD BANK to complete the puzzle.

WORD BANK

alimentary canal	amniotic	fracture	testes	bladder
palm	hinge	alignment	tendons	pelvis
humerus	skeleton	cervix	epidermis	enamel
pulse	pituitary	excretory	sebum	
pancreas	genes			
pressure point	adrenal			
heart	ovaries			

ACROSS:

1. Outer layer of skin
4. The blood pump
6. Stores urine
10. The "bite" is the _____ of the teeth
11. Opening to the uterus
12. Boney structure
13. The inside of the hand
14. Controls body growth and other glands
17. A break in a bone
20. Rhythm of the heart creates a _____
21. Female sex glands
22. Determine human traits

DOWN:

1. Waste removal system
2. Outer layer of the tooth
3. Upper arm bone
5. Gland that goes to work when we are excited, angry, or frightened
7. Fluid surrounding fetus
8. Long food tube
9. Joint found in elbow
12. Oily substance given off by the sebaceous gland
13. Gland which controls the body's use of glucose
15. Place by or beside a wound to stop bleeding
16. Muscles are attached to the skeleton by _____
18. Male sex glands
19. Framework of bones that supports lower part of abdomen

Name

Directions: Make an **X** in the correct box to show to which system/systems each organ belongs. One is done for you.

ORGANS	SYSTEMS						
	Digestive	Respiratory	Urinary	Reproductive	Circulatory	Nervous	Endocrine
Bladder			X				
Brain							
Heart							
Ovaries							
Liver							
Pancreas							
Kidney							
Spinal Cord							
Lungs							
Small Intestines							
Diaphragm							
Mouth							
Nerves							
Testes							
Thyroid Gland							
Arteries							
Esophagus							
Cerebellum							

Name _____

All kinds of traits are inherited: the shape of your nose, the color of your hair, the shape of your body. Many of these traits cannot be changed. Your inherited characteristics are inborn and make you the way you are. Other traits, such as intelligence, personality, and learned abilities, may be inherited to a certain extent but are greatly influenced by your environment and your attitudes toward them. Your mother may have been a talented soccer player and your father a world-class wrestler, but you will not be either unless you choose to put in many long hours of practice.

Which of the following characteristics are inherited? Which of the following characteristics can be changed by your behavior?

Directions: Mark a **U** beside the things that cannot be changed and a **C** beside the things that can be changed.

1. _____ your ability to learn spelling words

2. _____ the shape of your feet

3. _____ your ability to ice skate

4. _____ the shape of your teeth

5. Now think about yourself and some of the characteristics you have—things you can change and things you cannot change. Write two paragraphs describing yourself in terms of the characteristics you have thought about.

_____

_____

_____

_____

_____

_____

_____

_____

6. Why do you think it is important to know whether a trait is inherited?

_____

_____

_____

Name _____

The mirror in your bathroom gives you a reflected image of what you look like. You look the way you do because of your cells and genes. Although we don't really know how many cells make up a human body, it is estimated that our bodies contain 50–100 trillion cells. A **cell** is the basic unit of a living thing that performs all of the functions of life. Each cell contains a special unit called a gene. A **gene** is an inherited unit of genetic material found within a cell that determines a trait. Some of the traits we inherit can be seen while others cannot. Traits we can see include the color of our hair and eyes, the shape of our noses, and our build.

You inherited your genes from your parents. Your parents inherited their genes from their parents, and so on. Genetic material is passed from one generation to the next. You get half of your genes from your mother, and half from your father. It takes at least two genes to determine a single trait—one comes from your mother and the other one comes from your father. If your mother has brown eyes and your father has blue eyes, then you inherit a gene for brown eyes from your mother and a gene for blue eyes from your father. But the gene for blue eyes is not as strong as the gene for brown eyes. We call this weaker gene a recessive gene. We call the stronger gene a dominant gene. Because the brown eye gene is stronger than the blue eye gene, you will have two brown eyes.

Directions: Use the information to answer the following questions.

1. What is a cell? _____

2. What is a gene? _____

3. What are some other traits not mentioned above that people inherit? _____

    _____

4. How many genes determine a single trait? _____

    From where do they come? _____

5. Why are there more people with brown eyes than blue eyes? _____

    _____

6. Curly hair is a dominant trait. If you inherited a gene for curly hair from your mother and a gene for straight hair from your father, would you have straight or curly hair? Why?

    _____

    _____

    _____

A Special Science Tool

The microscope is a necessary tool when observing tiny organisms in life science. In about 1590, two Dutch spectacle makers, Hans and Zaccharias Janssen, started experimenting with lenses. They put several lenses in a tube and made a very important discovery. The object near the end of the tube appeared to be greatly enlarged! They had just invented the compound microscope.

Other people heard of the Janssen's work and started work of their own. Galileo added a focusing device. Anthony Leeuwenhoek of Holland became so interested that he learned how to make lenses. By grinding and polishing, he was able to make small lenses with great curvatures. These rounder lenses produced greater magnification, and his microscopes were able to magnify up to 270 times.

Anthony Leeuwenhoek's new, improved microscope allowed people to see things no human had ever seen before. He saw bacteria, yeast, and blood cells. Because of his great contributions, he has been called the "Father of Microscopy."

Robert Hooke, an Englishman, also spent much of his life working with microscopes and improved their design and capabilities. He coined the word *cell* after observing cork cells under a microscope. He was reminded of a monk's cell in a monastery.

Little was done to improve the microscope until the middle of the 19th century, when great strides were made and quality instruments such as today's microscope emerged.

Directions: Use the words from the WORD BANK and a science resource book to help you label this microscope.

WORD BANK

eyepiece
fine adjustment
stage
mirror
body tube
objective
stage clips
diaphragm
coarse adjustment
arm
base
nosepiece

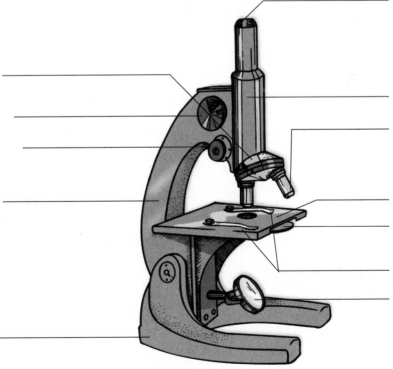

Name

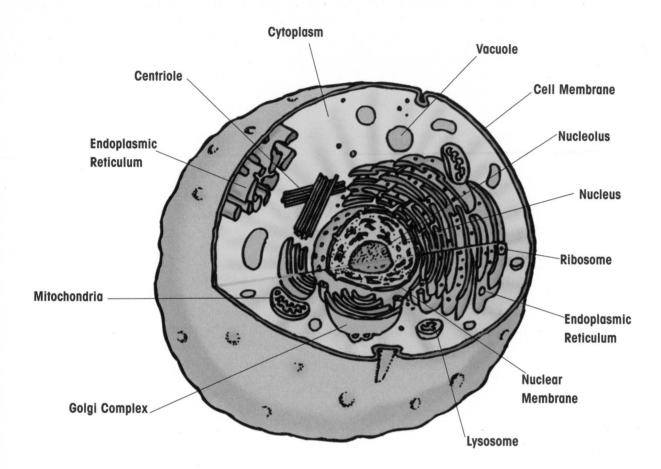

Cytoplasm

Vacuole

Centriole

Cell Membrane

Endoplasmic
Reticulum

Nucleolus

Nucleus

Ribosome

Mitochondria

Endoplasmic
Reticulum

Nuclear
Membrane

Golgi Complex

Lysosome

Vacuole—contains water and dissolved minerals

Lysosome—digests large particles

Ribosomes—where proteins are made

Golgi Complex—stores and releases chemicals

Cytoplasm—jelly-like substance within the cell

Nucleus—chromosomes are found here

Nucleolus—spherical body within the nucleus

Nuclear Membrane—holds nucleus together

Cell Membrane—controls entry into and out of the cell

Mitochondria—releases energy from the nutrients

Endoplasmic Reticulum—surface for chemical activity

Centriole—structures involved in mitosis in animal cells only

Plant Cell

All living things are made of cells. Some organisms, such as the paramecium and the amoeba, have one cell, while others, such as the human, have millions of cells. Each type of cell has its own function. Plant cells have different functions than human muscle cells, for example. Look at the diagrams below and on the next page. They show similarities and differences between a plant cell and an animal cell. Be sure to read the descriptions of the parts of the cell.

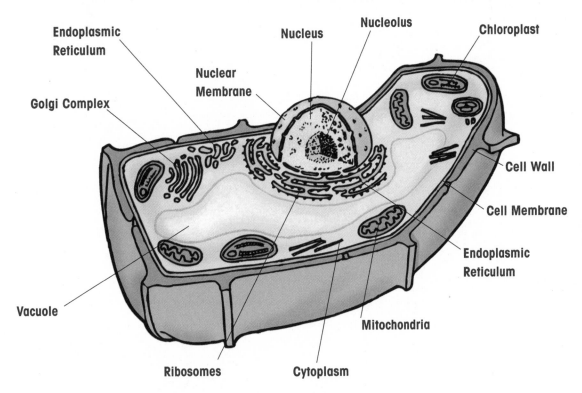

Ribosomes—where proteins are made

Golgi Complex—stores and releases chemicals

Cytoplasm—jelly-like substance within the cell

Nucleus—chromosomes are found here

Nucleolus—spherical body within the nucleus

Nuclear Membrane—holds nucleus together

Mitochondria—releases energy from the nutrients

Cell Wall—shapes and supports a plant cell

Vacuole—contains water and dissolved minerals

Chloroplast—food for plant cells is made here

Cell Membrane—controls entry into and out of the cell

Endoplasmic Reticulum—surface for chemical activity

Each small part of the cell is called an *organelle*. Each organelle has its own name and function. Many of the organelles in a plant cell are also in an animal cell.

What's the Difference?

Name

Directions: Look at the diagrams and descriptions of the animal and plant cells on pages 34–35.

1. Write about the differences that are obvious between the two cells. Think about why many parts are the same, and write about why you think that might be.

2. What might plants be like if their cells had no chloroplast? How might it make a difference?

3. Why do you think plant cells have cell walls instead of cell membranes? Why do you think animal cells have cell membranes instead of cell walls?

4. Do you think plant or animal cells use more energy to live? Why?

Name _____

Directions: Use the reading selection and the diagrams on pages 34–35 to define the following terms.

1. Ribosomes _____

   _____

2. Cytoplasm _____

   _____

3. Nucleus _____

   _____

4. Nuclear Membrane _____

   _____

5. Mitochondria _____

   _____

6. Cell Membrane _____

   _____

7. Golgi Complex _____

   _____

8. Vacuole _____

   _____

Directions: Now, use the words above to complete the following sentences.

1. The _____ holds the cell together.

2. The _____, organelles specific to green plants, contain the chemical chlorophyll, which permits a green plant to produce its own sugar.

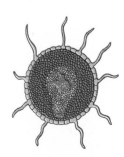

Animal or Plant?

Most scientists divide all living things into five groups, called **kingdoms**. Two of the largest are the Animal Kingdom and the Plant Kingdom.

Directions: Compare these two kingdoms by using the chart below. Check the correct box or boxes next to each characteristic.

CHARACTERISTIC	PLANT	ANIMAL
Living organisms		
Formed from cells		
Cells have chlorophyll		
Makes its own food		
Gets food from outside		
Moves from place to place		
Has limited movement		
Can reproduce its own kind		
Depends on sun's energy		

The whole ecology of a given location on the earth can become unbalanced with the disappearance of just a single creature. This is because of a system called the **food chain**. The food chain is a concept that was developed by a scientist named Charles Elton. In 1927, he laid out the process by which plants get their energy from the sunlight, plant-eating animals get their energy from eating plants, and meat-eating animals get their energy from other animals. Seen in black and white, this looks very much like a chain, with its links all together.

Let's look at the food chain more closely. The food chain has four basic parts.

- The first part is the **sun**. The sun provides the energy for everything on the earth.

- The second part is known as **producers**. Producers are all green plants. They make their own food, and every organism is in part dependent on plants for the oxygen and/or food they need.

- **Consumers** are the third part of the food chain. Consumers are, very simply, every organism that eats something else, whether it is a **carnivore** (eats meat), an **herbivore** (eats plants), an **omnivore** (eats plants and animals), a **parasite** (relies on another living thing to provide food), or a **scavenger** (usually feeds on dead organisms).

- The fourth part of the food chain is **decomposers**. These organisms, such as fungi and bacteria, break down dead matter into important gases that are released back into the ground, air, or water. These "recycled" nutrients are then used by the producers in their growth process.

Look at the simplified food chain on the right. The sunlight helps the grass to grow, the rabbit eats the grass, and the fox eats the rabbit. Because the fox does not have a predator, it is the "top" of this food chain.

If something happens to the grass—perhaps a drought occurs—and the rabbits have less food, many may die. Without as many rabbits to eat, some of the foxes in the area may also die or leave the location. While this is a very simple look at the food chain (because rabbits do eat things other than grass), you can see that the disappearance of one element in the chain can have a lasting effect.

39

Name _____

The term **food web** describes the many interlocking food chains in an area somewhere on the earth or in the water. Look at the food web below. Notice how the crops are eaten by humans, birds, aphids, and crickets or how the cricket is eaten by the chameleon and the frog. This shows very clearly how one food chain relies on another. It also shows how the failing of one element in a food chain might affect all living things in a location.

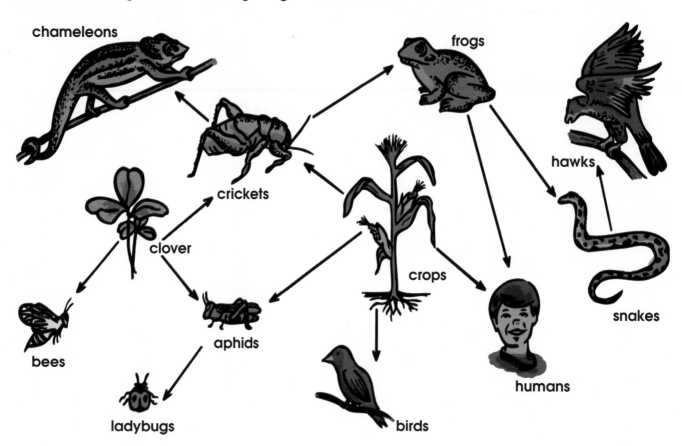

By breaking one link in an existing food chain, we run the risk of threatening all of the organisms above that one link, as well as other chains in a large food web. And this has happened many times. One example is the use of the pesticide DDT in the 1960s. This pesticide was very effective in helping to eliminate certain insects. But as it washed off the plants and out of the soil into the water supply, plankton and other small organisms took in the DDT. These organisms were then eaten by small fish, resulting in the fish having the DDT in them. Larger fish and birds ate the smaller fish, and the birds were affected. Birds such as the osprey and eagle developed very thin eggshells and became threatened. This is known as the *domino effect*.

Name _____

Directions: Use the reading on pages 39–40 to help define the following terms.

1. Consumers _____

   _____

2. Producers _____

   _____

3. Sun _____

   _____

4. Pesticides _____

   _____

5. Food chain _____

   _____

6. Food web _____

   _____

7. Domino effect _____

   _____

8. Energy _____

   _____

Directions: Now, answer the following questions.

1. What term means that the "death of one species in a food chain upsets the rest of the food chain"? _____

   _____

2. Look at the food web on page 40. Describe several different food chains in the web.

   _____

   _____

   _____

   _____

   _____

Eating would be boring if we ate only one kind of food. Imagine eating only pizza for breakfast, lunch, and dinner, 365 days a year, for the rest of your life. Most animals, like humans, eat more than one type of food. This means that most animals are members of more than one food chain. Separate food chains that interlock are called food webs.

Directions: Form a food web by drawing arrows from each prey to its predator. Remember that most prey have more than one predator. Use a different color crayon for each food chain.

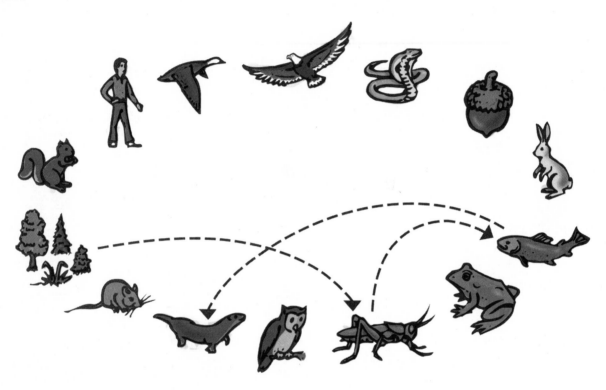

One food chain that you may have found in the web is this one:

plant ⟶ **grasshopper** ⟶ **fish** ⟶ **otter**

Directions: Now, write one more food chain you can find.

_____

_____

_____

Name _____

Looking closely at the information on a cereal box, you can learn many interesting things about the product.

Directions: Carefully read the information on the illustration of the cereal box. Answer the questions. Compare these answers with the information found on a box of cereal you might eat for breakfast.

	CORN BALLS	YOUR CEREAL
What kind of grain(s) is used?		
Is sugar used?		
What position is sugar on the list of ingredients?		
List other sweeteners.		
How many calories per serving without milk?		
How many calories per serving when eaten with 1/2 cup of skim milk?		
How much protein per serving?		
How many vitamins and minerals does the cereal contain?		
How much cholesterol is in one serving?		
How much fat is in one serving?		
How much carbohydrate is in one serving?		

NUTRITION INFORMATION

SERVING SIZE: 1 OZ. (28.4 g, ABOUT 1 CUP)
CORN BALLS ALONE OR WITH 1/2 CUP
VITAMINS A AND D SKIM MILK.
SERVINGS PER PACKAGE: 15

	CEREAL	WITH 1/2 CUP VITAMINS A & D SKIM MILK
CALORIES	110	150*
PROTEIN	1 g	5 g
CARBOHYDRATE	26 g	32 g
FAT	0 g	0 g*
CHOLESTEROL	0 mg	0 mg*
SODIUM	90 mg	150 mg
POTASSIUM	20 mg	220 mg

PERCENTAGE OF U.S. RECOMMENDED DAILY ALLOWANCES (U.S. RDA)

PROTEIN	2	10
VITAMIN A	15	20
VITAMIN C	25	25
THIAMIN	25	30
RIBOFLAVIN	25	35
NIACIN	25	25
CALCIUM	**	15
IRON	10	10
VITAMIN D	10	25
VITAMIN B$_6$	25	25
ZINC	10	15

* WHOLE MILK SUPPLIES AN ADDITIONAL 30
  CALORIES. 4g. FAT, AND 15mg CHOLESTEROL.
** CONTAINS LESS THAN 2% OF THE U.S. RDA
  OF THIS NUTRIENT.

INGREDIENTS: CORN, SUGAR, CORN SYRUP, MOLASSES, SALT, ANNATTO COLOR,

VITAMINS AND MINERALS: VITAMIN C (SODIUM ASCORBATE AND ASCORBIC ACID), NIACINAMIDE, ZINC (OXIDE), IRON, VITAMIN B6 (PYRIDOXINE HYDROCHLORIDE), VITAMIN B2 (RIBOFLAVIN), VITAMIN A (PALMITATE; PROTECTED WITH BHT), VITAMIN B1 (THIAMIN HYDROCHLORIDE), FOLIC ACID, AND VITAMIN D.

43 *Science: Grade 6*

An **environment** includes all living and nonliving things with which an organism interacts. These living and nonliving things are **interdependent**; that is, they depend on one another. The living things in an environment (plants, animals) are called **biotic factors**, and the nonliving things (soil, light, temperature) are called **abiotic factors**. **Ecology** is the study of the relationships and interactions of living things with one another and their environment.

Living things inhabit many different environments. A group of organisms living and interacting with each other in their nonliving environment is called an **ecosystem**. The different organisms that live together in an ecosystem are called a **community**. Within a community, each kind of living thing (i.e., frogs) makes up a **population**.

Directions: Study the picture. Follow the directions.

1. Label two biotic factors and two abiotic factors in the picture.

2. Explain the relationships among the living things in the pictured environment. _____

   _____

3. Name the type of ecosystem pictured. _____

4. Circle all the members of the community.

5. Explain how the organisms in this environment are dependent upon one another. _____

   _____

6. List the different kinds of populations that live in the environment. _____

   _____

Name _____

Most of the living things in your neighborhood can be classified into one of two main groups—plants and animals. Plants and animals are classified, or compared to something else, based on their physical structure and behavior. Each different kind of plant and animal is known as a **species**. A group of the same species is called a **population**.

Populations of living things live in an **ecosystem**, an area in which living things interact with each other and their environment. Like neighborhoods, ecosystems can be very small or extremely large. Within each ecosystem, there may be many different habitats. A **habitat** is the place where a population normally lives in an ecosystem. The habitat must supply the needs of organisms, such as food, water, temperature, oxygen, and minerals. If the population's needs are not met, it will either move to a better habitat or die out.

Different populations need different habitats. A population of fish needs a body of water. A population of monkeys needs a jungle. Habitats can be shared. When several populations share a habitat, it is called a **community**. All of the populations living in the community work together to meet their needs.

If something in the community changes, such as the population of fish in a lake increasing, then another population, such as the insects, may become endangered. If conditions do not change or the habitat vanishes, then all of the members of the population may die and the species may become extinct.

Directions: Use the information to answer the following questions.

1. What are the two main groups of living things? _____

2. How are they classified? _____

3. How are an ecosystem, a habitat, and a community alike? _____

    _____

    How are they different? _____

4. What needs of a living thing does a habitat supply? _____

    _____

    _____

5. What happens if a habitat cannot supply the needs named in question 4?

    _____

    _____

Name _____

On your way to school, did you walk or drive through a neighborhood? Did you see houses or businesses? Did you see people, animals, trees, and grass? These are all part of that one neighborhood. An ecosystem is similar to a neighborhood. It is the whole community of living and nonliving things. All of these things exist together and interact with one another.

Ecosystems can be on land or water. They are all different from one another for many reasons. Those reasons include the amount of water in an area, the type of soil, and the kinds of plants and animals that live there.

Directions: Look at the two ecosystems. Compare the two. Name three differences.

_____

_____

_____

_____

_____

_____

_____

Habitats Recall

Directions: Circle the correct answers.

1. A habitat is a(n)

   a. action we do everyday.

   b. location where specific animals and plants live and interact.

   c. specific weather pattern.

2. Living organisms are one of three things that help maintain the balance in an ecosystem. They can be

   a. producers, consumers, or decomposers.

   b. plants, trees, or grass.

   c. animals, plants, or rocks.

3. Succession is the process of change in the plants and animals of a community over a period of time.

   true or false

4. Ecology is the study of

   a. living things and what they eat.

   b. animals that live and grow.

   c. living things and their environment.

5. A group of _____ and _____ things interacting with each other is considered an ecosystem.

   a. living, nonliving

   b. moving, growing

   c. habitat, plant

Directions: Use complete sentences to answer the following question.

Think about the impact of humans on natural habitats. Write a position statement about your opinion on this issue. Your position could be against the destruction of habitats or for development that can lead to destruction of habitats.

_____

_____

_____

_____

_____

Do you have an apple at home? Ask an adult to cut it open. What do you see? The apple has layers. The top layer is the peel. It is thin but tough and protects the fruit. The next layer is the fruit. It can be soft or hard and most of the apple is the fruit. The inside layer is the core. It is harder than the rest of the apple and protects the seeds that are in the center.

The earth is very much like the apple. It has four layers. The outer layer is the **crust**. It is solid rock. The rock is from 5 to 20 miles thick, and is thicker underneath the continents. The next layer is called the **mantle**. It is the thickest layer, about 1,800 miles thick and made up of rock. This rock may move because of the high temperatures and great pressure found there. The third layer is the **outer core**. It is liquid, or melted iron. This layer is about 1,400 miles thick. The innermost layer is the **inner core**. It is made of iron and nickel. It is extremely hot, reaching temperatures of more than 9,000°F. This is a solid mass of rock and is about 800 miles thick.

Directions: Label the layers of the earth. Then, answer the questions.

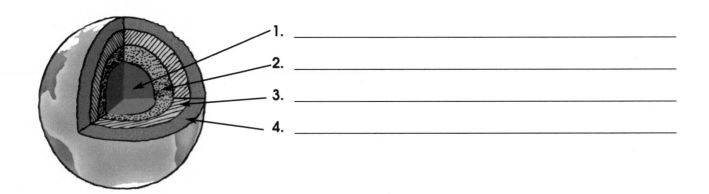

1. _____

2. _____

3. _____

4. _____

5. Which layer of the earth do you think shows the most evidence of an earthquake?

_____

_____

6. How do you think scientists find out about the inner cores of the earth?

_____

_____

Name _____

According to the theory of plate tectonics, the earth's crust is broken into about twenty plates. These **plates** are slowly moving. The edges of some of these plates are moving toward each other. A **trench** is formed when one plate bends and dives under another. These diving edges then descends into the earth's hot **mantle** and starts melting into **magma**. The magma can then rise and break through the earth's crust and burst out of a **volcano**. The edge of the above-riding plate crumples, resulting in a mountain range.

Directions: Label the diagram below.

WORD BANK

volcano	ocean	trench	magma
continent	descending plate	above-riding plate	

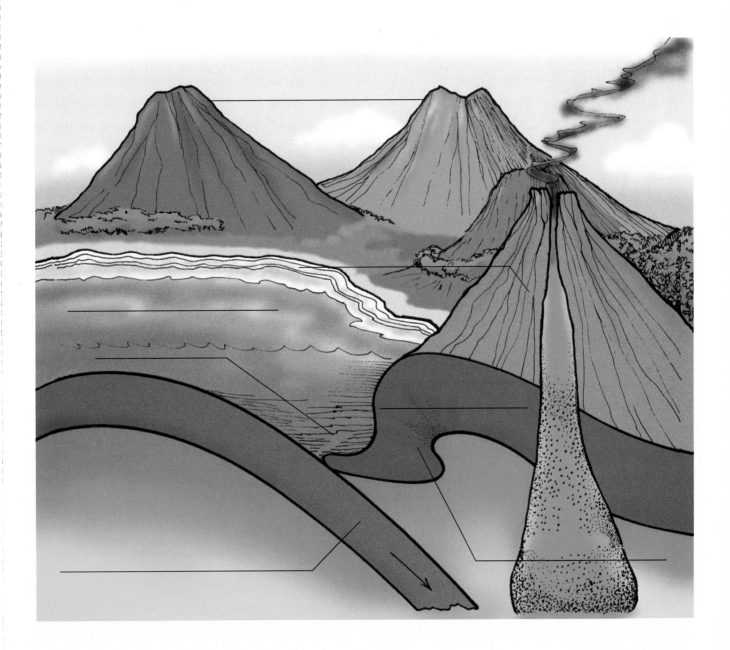

Name _____

The earth's crust is made of rigid plates that are always moving. The boundaries of some of these plates are along the edges of the continents, while others are in the middle of the ocean. The map on this page shows the major plates near North and South America.

Directions: Using an encyclopedia or some other source, label the eight plates pictured below.

WORD BANK

Gorda Plate	North American Plate	Cocos Plate
Pacific Plate	South American Plate	Nazca Plate
Antarctic Plate	Caribbean Plate	

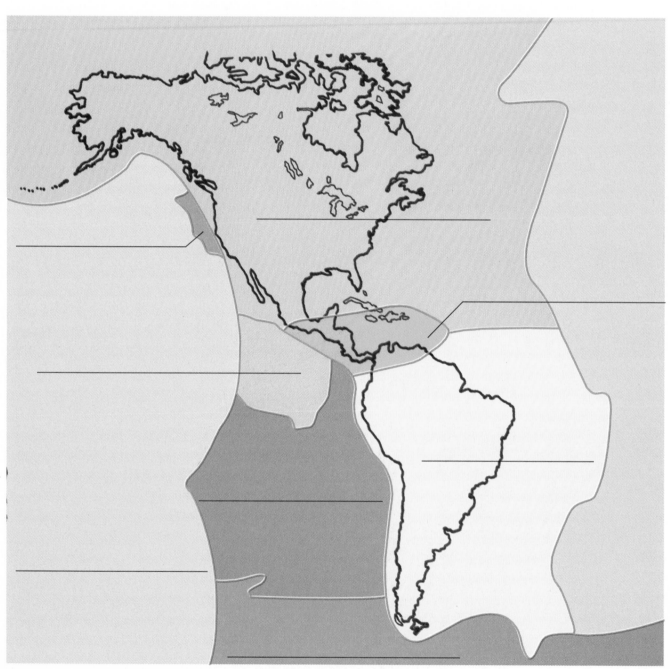

Name _____

The word **climate** is used to describe the weather in a particular place over a long period of time. Because the United States covers such a large area, it has a number of different climate zones. Some areas have long, cold winters and short, cool summers, while other areas are warm in both summer and winter.

WORD BANK

1 ☐ alpine   5 ☐ desert   9 ☐ tropical
2 ☐ steppe   6 ☐ continental   10 ☐ subarctic
3 ☐ tundra   7 ☐ subtropical
4 ☐ mediterranean   8 ☐ marine

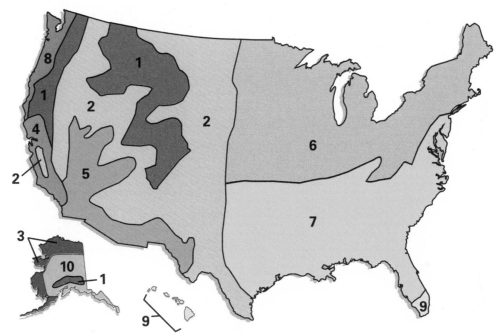

Directions: Choose colors to color-code the Map Key and the climate zone map. Then, determine the . . .

climate zone you live in. _____

climate zone of the Northeast. _____

climate zone of the Rocky Mountains. _____

climate zones found in Alaska. _____

climate zones found in Texas. _____

climate zones of Florida. _____

climate zone of Michigan. _____

The names of clouds come from Latin words that describe their appearance. Here are five words that are used alone or in combination to name the basic cloud types.

Cirrus   feathery (from Latin *cirrus*, meaning "curl, filament, tuft")

Cumulus   piled up (from Latin *cumulus*, meaning "heap, mass")

Stratus   sheet (from Latin *stratus*, meaning "stretched out, extended")

Nimbus   rain (from Latin *nimbus*, meaning "heavy rain; rain cloud")

Alto   high (from Latin *altus*, meaning "high")

The names of the ten basic cloud types use these words alone or in combination.

Directions: See if you can figure out what each of these clouds looks like from its name.

1. Cirrus clouds are _____

2. Cirrocumulus clouds are _____

3. Cirrostratus clouds are _____

4. Altocumulus clouds are _____

5. Altostratus clouds are _____

6. Nimbostratus clouds are _____

7. Stratus clouds are _____

8. Stratocumulus clouds are _____

9. Cumulus clouds are _____

10. Cumulonimbus clouds are _____

Name _____

Directions: Using what you have learned about cloud shapes and altitudes, label the clouds in the chart below.

 WORD BANK

Altocumulus (Ac)
Cumulus (Cu)
Cirrostratus (Cs)
Stratus (St)

Cirrocumulus (Cc)
Stratocumulus (Sc)
Cumulonimbus (Cb)

Cirrus (Ci)
Altostratus (As)
Nimbostratus (Ns)

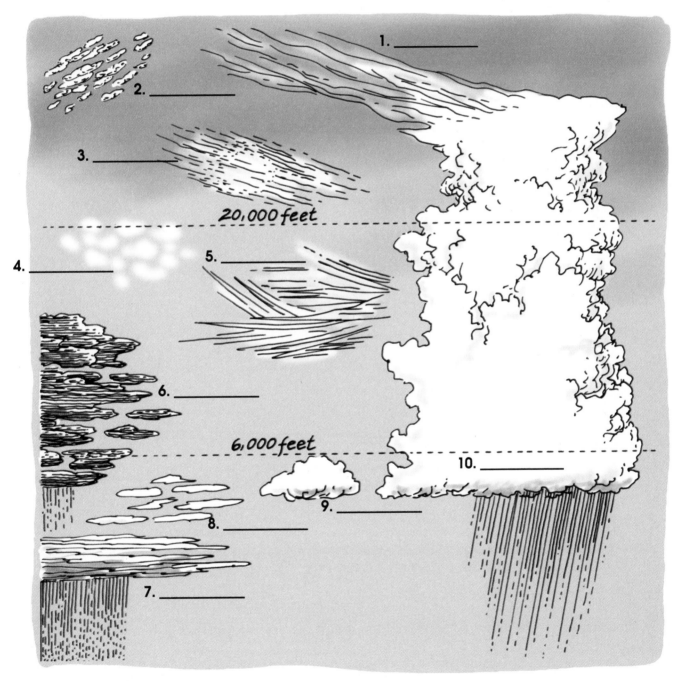

1. _____

2. _____

3. _____

20,000 feet

4. _____

5. _____

6. _____

6,000 feet

7. _____

8. _____

9. _____

10. _____

A Magic Square of Weather

Name

Below are words relating to weather.

Directions: Write the number of the word which fits a clue in a box on the grid. If you have matched the correct numbers in all 16 squares, the sums of the rows, columns, and diagonals will be the same. This is called a *magic square*.

1. atmosphere	5. jet streams	9. wind	13. land breeze
2. troposphere	6. stratosphere	10. greenhouse effect	14. doldrums
3. ionosphere	7. mesosphere	11. convection	15. trade winds
4. ozone	8. exosphere	12. sea breeze	16. front

mass of air that surrounds earth _____	air that rushes in from the north and south to warm the air along the equator _____	calm areas of earth where there is little wind _____	a gas in the upper part of earth's atmosphere _____
cold air from the ocean that moves into the warmer land _____	the zone of the atmosphere above the troposphere _____	the zone of the atmosphere above the stratosphere _____	a movement of air close to earth's surface _____
the outer zone of earth's atmosphere _____	air above earth that is warmed by the reflection of the sun's rays and is prevented from easily passing back into space _____	transfer of heat by currents of air or water _____	strong, steady winds high in the atmosphere; used by pilots _____
cold air from land that moves out to warmer air over oceans _____	zone of the atmosphere which affects the transmission of radio waves _____	the zone of the atmosphere which is closest to the surface of earth _____	the line along which air masses meet _____

What is the magic number for this puzzle? _____

Can you discover other number combinations in the puzzle which give you the same answer?

_____

_____

54

Symbol Sense

Forecasters use symbols to show others their weather predictions. These symbols are often used in television and newspaper forecasts. How well do you know these symbols?

Directions: The boxes below contain 12 standard weather symbols plus four "fake" symbols. At the bottom of the page are descriptions of the symbols, but there are two extra symbols. First, cross out the fake symbols. Then, match the real symbols with their correct labels by writing the number of each in a blank by its label. Finally, cross out the two extra symbols.

_____	A. thunderstorm	_____	H. cold front
_____	B. fog	_____	I. 1/2 cloud
_____	C. calm	_____	J. snow
_____	D. missing data	_____	K. no cloud
_____	E. wind direction and speed	_____	L. rain shower
_____	F. drizzle	_____	M. mist
_____	G. warm front	_____	N. high pressure system

Read the brief history of the naming of hurricanes below. Then, place the hurricanes that follow in their proper time frame.

THE HISTORY OF NAMING HURRICANES IN AMERICA

Hurricanes that strike the Atlantic Basin are given names to expedite communication about their paths and development, but this was not always the case. Storms in early America were identified only by their latitude and longitude. The general names they were assigned which made reference to related events, places, or persons were created only after the storms had passed, so historians talk of the Charleston Hurricane of 1811 or the Benjamin Franklin Eclipse Hurricane, but those who lived through the storms knew them only by their locations.

Identifying a hurricane by its longitude and latitude became cumbersome and prone to error when radio communications and forecasting methods made it possible to warn residents of an approaching storm. So, air force and navy meteorologists began identifying storms with female names during World War II. Meteorologist Clement Wragge had already begun this tradition in Australia 50 years earlier, and author George R. Steward had, too, in his 1941 novel called *Storm*.

Still the United States weather services did not start naming storms until 1950, when they experimented with assigning names according to the phonetic alphabet (Able, Baker, Charlie, etc.). In 1953 they abandoned that failed experiment for the less confusing use of female names to identify hurricanes in America. In 1978 they added male names to the array.

Today, scientists have devised a six-year rotation of hurricane names. The first storm of a season takes on the name that begins with *A* for that year, the second storm takes on the name that begins with *B*, etc. Since the names cycle through a six-year rotation, the first four storms of the year 2000, for example, were called Alberto, Beryl, Chris, and Debby, just as the first four of 1994 were named. Once a hurricane has caused enormous damage, its name is retired and a new one takes its place.

Directions: Identify the proper time period for each of the following storms according to the name it claims. The first one has been done for you.

 WORD BANK

Hurricane Easy	1860—Hurricane I	Hurricane Audrey
The Great Hurricane of 1780	Hurricane King	Hurricane George
Hurricane Hugo	Hurricane Able	Hurricane Mitch
The Late Gale at St. Joseph	Hurricane Hazel	Hurricane Eloise

BEFORE 1950	1950 – 1952	1952 – 1978	1978 – PRESENT
1860 – Hurricane I			

 Science: Grade 6

Defining Droughts

Directions: Drought is a relative term, and scientists do not agree on a single definition for the word. Read some of the drought definitions below and then answer the questions that follow.

DROUGHT DEFINITIONS

#1: Wayne Palmer of the National Weather Service devised a drought index that compares precipitation and stored soil moisture with evaporation and a region's requirements for moisture. According to a formula, the drought index defines a water balance between -2 and +2 as normal, a balance between -2 and -3 as a moderate drought, a balance between -3 and -4 as a severe drought, and a balance of 4 or below as an extreme drought.

#2: Scientists in Great Britain define an absolute drought as a period of 15 consecutive days in which each day received less than .01 inches of rain. They consider 29 consecutive days with a mean daily average rainfall less than .01 a partial drought.

#3: In India a drought is declared when the annual rainfall is 75% less than average.

#4: Libya does not declare a drought until it has experienced no rain for two years.

#5: The Swedish hydrologist Malin Falkenmark created the following definition of dry climates:
Aridity—permanently dry climate
Drought—irregularly dry climate
Desiccation—dry soils due to overgrazing and deforestation
Water Stress—water shortages due to a growing population relying on a fixed supply of run-off water

#6: One operational definition of drought categorizes a dry spell into its effects, defining a meteorological drought according to degree and duration of dryness, an agricultural drought as one that affects agriculture, a hydrological drought as one that affects the hydrologic system, and a socioeconomic drought as one that affects supply and demand of commodities necessary to human life.

_____ Which two definitions would be most helpful in directing national policy on agriculture and population growth?

_____ Which definition would be most helpful to scientists who wish to quantify drought seasons for comparative purposes?

_____ Which definition would probably be most simply explained to everyday citizens?

_____ Which definition considers dry conditions a drought only if those conditions are abnormal to a region?

_____ Which definition associates a specific quantity of rainfall with the term *drought*?

_____ Which definition considers how much rainfall an area needs in determining the existence of a drought?

_____ Which three definitions consider the length of a dry spell in their definitions of drought?

_____ Which definition considers the causes of a region's dry spells and water shortages?

What Are You Wearing?

Did your teacher suggest you wear your jacket on the playground? Are you wishing you had shorts on? Are the slides too hot to slide down? The answers to these questions often can be answered by thinking about the **weather**. Weather is the condition of the air surrounding us. Scientists talk about four properties of air when they speak about the weather. They are air temperature, air pressure, wind, and humidity.

Air temperature is determined by the sun. The sun's energy heats up the earth and the surface warms the air above it. Air temperature is measured using a thermometer.

Air pressure is the amount of force that air is pushing on something. Warm air is lighter and gives less pressure. The air particles are farther apart than in cool air. Air pressure is measured using a barometer.

Wind is air in motion. It is caused when the surface of the earth heats unevenly. The air will move from high pressure to low pressure. This results in the movement of air, or wind. Scientists measure wind using an anemometer.

Humidity is how much water vapor is in the air. The presence of water vapor depends on location. If you are near a large body of water you may experience more humid air. The humidity is measured with a hygrometer.

Directions: Answer the following questions using the information above.

1. What are the four properties of air used to describe weather?

   _____

   _____

2. Describe what you might wear on the playground if it was hot and humid.

   _____

   _____

3. What are a barometer and an anemometer used to measure?

   _____

   _____

4. Describe what the weather is like on your playground today and what is was like yesterday.

   _____

   _____

   _____

 Science: Grade 6

Name

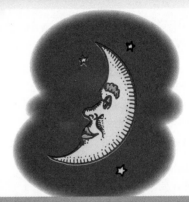

As you travel to school, look up. What do you see? Perhaps it is a clear blue sky. Maybe it is cloudy and rainy. It might even still be early enough for you to see the moon. The moon is the earth's nearest neighbor in space. Have you ever thought about the moon? What is it like? Is it important to us?

Look at the chart below. It has some information comparing the earth and moon.

EARTH	MOON
1. Atmosphere is a combination of gases, such as water vapor and oxygen	1. Little or no atmosphere
2. Surface has liquid water and life	2. Dusty and lifeless on surface
3. Gravity is six times stronger than moon	3. Weak gravitational pull
4. Earth revolves around the sun in 365 days	4. Moon revolves around the earth in about 28 days
5. Many landforms including mountains, rivers, and plains	5. Landforms include mountains, plains, and craters
6. Diameter of 7,926 mi.	6. Diameter of 2,160 mi.
7. 5th largest planet, 3rd from the sun	7. Natural satellite orbiting the earth

Directions: Use the chart to answer the following questions.

1. Which is larger, the earth or moon? How do you know? _____

   _____

2. Describe what you think the surface of the earth is like compared to the moon's surface.

   _____

   _____

3. What four events occur as a result of the earth's revolving around the sun every 365 days?

   _____

   _____

Name _____

How far around the sun can you walk in one minute in each planet's orbit? Compare the distances.

	Mercury	Venus	Earth	Mars	Jupiter	Saturn	Uranus	Neptune	Pluto
Average Distance to Sun (Millions of Miles)	36	67	93	142	484	885	1,781	2,788	3,660
Scale Distance (Feet)	1.80	3.34	4.66	7.12	24.17	44.31	89.54	139.76	183.38
Your Scale Distance									

Directions: Answer the questions.

1. What did you notice about the distances of the inner planets from the sun compared to the outer planets' distances from the sun?

   _____

   _____

2. Describe what happened to the distance you traveled around the sun on each planet's orbit as you got further away from the sun.

   _____

   _____

3. Why do you think it takes a longer period of time for Pluto and Neptune to travel around the sun than it does for Mercury?

   _____

   _____

4. If it takes longer for the outer planets to travel around the sun, what happened to the length of each planet's year? Explain your answer.

   _____

   _____

   _____

Name _____

Several astronomical definitions appear below. The terms for each also appear below, but each has been altered.

Directions: Your job is to properly change each term and match it to the correct definition. To do this, change just one letter in each word and then rearrange the letters. The first one has been solved as an example.

	New Word	Definition	
1. heard	_____	__K__	A. Any body that revolves around the sun
2. square	_____	_____	B. A planet's natural satellite
3. slurps	_____	_____	C. A "shooting star"
4. riots	_____	_____	D. An extremely bright, compact object far beyond our galaxy
5. mask	_____	_____	E. The star nearest earth
6. pleats	_____	_____	F. Collapsed neutron star that emits pulsing radio waves
7. loom	_____	_____	G. A heavenly body with a star-like head and often with a long, luminous tail
8. ants	_____	_____	H. The path of a heavenly body revolving around another
9. bus	_____	_____	I. The imaginary line around which a body rotates
10. metro	_____	_____	J. A sphere of matter held together by its own gravitational field and generating nuclear fusion reactions in its interior
11. taxi	_____	_____	K. The third planet from the sun
12. remove	_____	_____	L. Nicknamed the "red planet"

Facts About Light Energy

Light energy is also called radiant energy. This kind of energy includes infrared rays, radio waves, ultraviolet rays, and X-rays.

Directions: Place a **T** before each true statement and an **F** before each false statement about light energy.

_____ 1. People can see the ultraviolet rays of the electromagnetic spectrum.

_____ 2. Radar is an instrument that uses radio waves to detect objects.

_____ 3. The longest wavelength of visible light is violet.

_____ 4. Infrared lamps are used to keep food warm in a restaurant.

_____ 5. Laser beams have one wavelength and travel in one direction.

_____ 6. Ultraviolet rays help people produce vitamin D.

_____ 7. X-rays are used to examine luggage at an airport.

_____ 8. Microwaves are used to fast-cook foods.

_____ 9. The number of waves passing one point in a second is called a *crest*.

_____ 10. Radio waves have the shortest wavelength.

_____ 11. Radio waves are used to broadcast television programs.

_____ 12. Cameras can record the infrared waves from people and animals.

_____ 13. The shortest wavelength of visible light is violet.

_____ 14. Gamma rays have the shortest wavelength and the highest energy.

_____ 15. Visible light is made up of a spectrum of colors.

_____ 16. Red-orange-yellow-green-blue-indigo-violet is the correct order of colors in the spectrum of visible light.

_____ 17. The distance from one wave crest to the next is called the *trough*.

_____ 18. A high-frequency wave has short wavelengths.

_____ 19. Microwaves can be seen by people.

_____ 20. Laser beams are often used at outdoor light shows.

_____ 21. Gamma rays are emitted by radioactive elements.

_____ 22. X-rays are used in medicine to locate broken bones.

Name _____

Directions: Use the terms in the WORD BANK to complete the statements relating to the behavior of light in the acrostic puzzle below.

WORD BANK

bent	flat	index	mirror	reflected
concave	focal	lens	photon	retina
convex	image	light	real image	virtual

1. When light travels from one medium to another, it is refracted, or ____ .

2. When rays of light strike and bounce off a mirror, the rays are ____ .

3. ____ is electromagnetic radiation and includes infrared, visible, and ultraviolet.

4. A ____ ____ can be projected on a screen.

5. A ____ image cannot be projected on a screen.

6. A ____ is a reflecting surface.

7. A ____ lens is thinner in the center than at the edges.

8. The back of the eye that receives an image is called the ____ .

9. A ____ lens is thicker in the center than at the edges.

10. The ____ point is the point at which light beams converge.

11. A ____ is a piece of glass or other transparent material which refracts light.

12. The ____ of refraction is the ratio of the speed of light in a vacuum to its speed in another medium.

13. A visual impression of an object in a mirror or through a lens is an ____ .

14. A ____ is a tiny package of electromagnetic energy.

15. A plane mirror is a ____ mirror.

1.   B __ __ __

2. __ __ __ __ E __ __ __ __ __

3. __ __ __ H __

4. __ __ __ __ __ A __ __

5. V __ __ __ __ __ __

6. __ I __ __ __ __

7. __ O __ __ __ __ __

8. R __ __ __ __ __

9. __ O __ __ __ __

10. F __ __ __ __

11. L __ __ __

12. I __ __ __ __

13. __ __ __ G __

14. __ H __ __ __ __

15. __ __ __ T

Name _____

Electricity is a very important form of energy. It produces light and heat, and provides power for household appliances and industrial machinery among many other things.

Directions: Rearrange the letters below to spell out words related to electricity.

1. TABETRY   _ _ _ _ E _ _

2. BLUB   _ _ L _

3. ESITRSRO   _ E _ _ _ _ _ _

4. HEGCAR   C _ _ _ _ _

5. DELETECRO   _ _ _ _ T _ _ _ _

6. TIURICC   _ _ R _ _ _ _

7. SUTILRONA   _ _ _ _ _ _ _ O _

8. NUCCODROT   _ _ N _ _ _ _ _

9. WIHCTS   S _ _ _ _ _

10. SOTEIVIP   _ O _ _ _ _ _ _

11. GANIVETE   N _ _ _ _ _ _ _

12. TWTA   _ _ T _

13. MOH   _ H _

14. SEUF   _ _ _ E

15. EMERAP   _ M _ _ _ _

16. NETROGERA   _ _ _ _ _ _ _ O _

17. TOVL   V _ _ _

18. RUTNIBE   _ _ _ _ _ _ E

Charge It

What makes your missing sock stick to the back of a shirt? What causes the shock and spark you get when you walk across the carpet and touch a doorknob? **Static electricity** is a form of electrical energy that is found freely in nature. Static electricity cannot run a television or turn on a light. But it can produce great bolts of lightning that light up the sky.

Matter is made of tiny particles called **atoms**. These particles are so small that we can't even see them with a regular microscope. Even though they're very small, atoms are made of even smaller particles. Some of these particles have a positive charge, and some have a negative charge. For atoms, opposites attract. Negative charges are attracted, or pulled, toward positive charges. The same charges (positive to positive and negative to negative) repel, or push away from each other. Positive and negative charges make your hair stand up when you take off a wool hat. The wool hat rubs against your hair. When you remove the hat, it takes some of the negatively charged particles that were in your hair. Your hair is left with a positive charge. Your hair stands up as its positive charges push away from one another.

Static electricity is an imbalance of positive and negative charges caused by **friction**, a force between two objects that are rubbing against one another. You might notice that your feet get warmer as you drag them across a carpeted floor. This is due to friction between your feet and the carpet. What you won't notice as you do this is that friction is causing negative particles to jump from the carpet to your socks. Touch a doorknob (a conductor) and ZAP! The negative charges from the carpet move through the doorknob to give you a shock.

Directions: Use the information above to answer the questions.

1. Where are positive and negative charges found? _____

2. Positive and negative charges _____ each other.

3. Two positive charges _____ each other.

4. What is static electricity? _____

5. What causes static electricity? _____

Name _____

Voltage is a measure of the force that pushes current through a conductor. It is expressed in volts. Circle the word **VOLT** in the grid. It may be written forward, backward, up, down, or diagonally.

How many volts can you find? _____

V	L	B	T	L	O	V	L	O	T	L	O	V
O	T	I	B	M	J	F	R	C	L	I	A	O
L	A	V	E	H	V	L	U	W	O	P	N	L
T	L	O	V	G	V	A	D	I	V	J	B	T
D	S	L	X	O	O	T	K	O	Z	M	L	O
Y	F	T	R	E	L	G	L	S	V	O	U	C
N	L	P	W	Y	T	T	L	O	V	X	Z	K
V	T	L	O	V	B	E	L	F	T	O	G	A
O	C	H	K	M	I	T	O	L	P	J	L	Q
R	V	O	L	T	S	V	Y	T	V	O	L	T
D	O	V	Z	W	V	O	C	N	E	A	U	L
V	L	F	J	H	O	L	M	B	T	R	D	O
O	T	N	V	X	L	T	P	L	G	L	Q	V
L	T	L	O	V	T	K	L	V	T	W	O	S
T	I	O	L	U	A	E	X	O	I	P	B	V
Y	C	F	T	H	K	T	L	O	V	R	O	D
V	O	L	T	Z	G	J	S	W	L	L	Q	O
T	N	Y	U	M	A	C	V	B	T	L	O	V

66

Newton's Laws

A scientist named Isaac Newton experimented and developed three laws of motion that hold true for matter on earth. The laws are as follows:

Law 1—An object in motion will remain in motion, and an object at rest will stay at rest unless a force acts on it.

Law 2—Acceleration of an object increases as the amount of force causing acceleration increases. The larger the mass of the item, the larger the force needed to result in acceleration.

Law 3—For every action there is an equal and opposite reaction.

These laws are at work everyday as you play on the playground. When you swing on the swing or kick the soccer ball to the net, you are experiencing Newton's laws.

Directions: Below are examples of motion on the playground. On the line next to the number, write the number of the law that is at work.

_____ **1.** You swing the baseball bat and hit the ball. It doesn't go as far as when the older boys hit the ball.

_____ **2.** You are standing on the merry-go-round waiting for someone to push it. When it does get pushed, you fall backward.

_____ **3.** You are playing marbles. You shoot one into another. The one you hit stops, but the one it hits moves out of the circle.

_____ **4.** You are in the school swimming pool gripping the edge. You push off the wall with your feet and shoot forward in the water.

_____ **5.** You are helping your teacher build a rock garden during recess. You are pushing a wheelbarrow full of rocks and then dump them. Pushing the wheelbarrow back to school is much easier.

Forms of Energy

Energy is what makes motion and change possible. It is the ability to do work. Energy is needed to make items move, from a car that takes you to school to your hair blowing in the breeze as you walk there. Energy is also needed to make matter change, such as when fire burns wood to ashes.

There are two types of energy. There is **kinetic energy**, which is energy that exists because something is moving, like a bus driving away from the bus stop. And there is **potential energy**, which is energy that exists because of its position. It gives the ability to do work in the future. This is like the car parked in the parking lot waiting to be turned on to take you to school.

Look at the pictures below. The one on the left shows potential energy. The rock can do work if it rolls down the hill. The one on the right shows kinetic energy. It is actually moving.

Potential

Kinetic

Directions: Decide if the statement is an example of potential or kinetic energy. Write **Potential** or **Kinetic** on the line. Then, draw an example of kinetic energy in the box.

_____ **1.** A bicycle locked in a bike rack

_____ **2.** The gym teacher jogging to school

_____ **3.** A wrecking ball breaking up the old school building

_____ **4.** The river you pass on the way to school

_____ **5.** Your dog watching you leave for school

_____ **6.** Your mother waving goodbye at the door

Gravity is the force which pulls all objects toward the earth. Some materials can insulate and cushion an object from the impact of gravity. Paper, foam cups, cloth, and similar materials are good insulators.

MATERIALS

Collect as many of these materials as possible before beginning the project:

- newspaper
- foam pieces or "peanuts,"
- pantyhose
- pieces of cloth
- string
- one or more raw eggs
- a shoe box or cardboard carton

PROCEDURE

The goal of this experiment is to have an egg survive from the highest possible height. Use the collected packaging materials to protect the egg inside the cardboard carton or shoe box. Be as creative as you can when wrapping the egg. Let an adult hold the package as high as possible or use a ladder to stand on. He or she will drop the package.

Check your egg. Did it break?

_____

If your egg didn't break the first time, have an adult drop it from a higher point. Did it break this time?

_____

From how high do you think the egg can be dropped before it breaks? _____

_____

69

Six Types of Simple Machines

Machines can increase or decrease a force, or they can change the amount of force needed to do work. There are six machines that are classified as simple machines.

Directions: Use the number pairs to identify the names of the six types of simple machines in the grid below. The horizontal number is first, and the vertical number is second. For example, the number pair 7-8 represents the letter *W*.

	1	2	3	4	5	6	7	8	9
9	E	G	A	D	U	H	C	N	L
8	B	F	Y	C	G	C	W	H	E
7	P	E	J	M	L	K	E	N	L
6	I	L	O	E	N	P	Q	D	R
5	L	R	N	D	S	N	L	T	W
4	A	E	A	Y	L	E	Z	R	E
3	U	X	V	L	A	C	E	E	I
2	S	D	W	F	D	I	P	B	X
1	W	V	G	E	J	A	H	L	K

___ ___ ___ ___ ___
4-3 7-7 2-1 1-9 8-4

___ ___ ___ ___ ___ ___ ___ ___   ___ ___ ___ ___ ___
9-3 3-5 6-8 1-5 6-2 8-9 2-4 5-2   7-2 9-9 3-4 6-5 2-7

___ ___ ___ ___ ___
1-2 4-8 9-6 4-6 3-2

___ ___ ___ ___ ___
7-8 4-1 8-6 2-9 8-3

___ ___ ___ ___ ___ ___
1-7 5-9 7-5 8-1 9-8 3-8

___ ___ ___ ___ ___   ___ ___ ___   ___ ___ ___ ___
1-1 6-9 6-4 9-4 5-7   1-4 5-6 4-5   6-1 9-2 2-6 7-3

Science: Grade 6

Page 6
The World of Arthropods

INSECTS—beetle, termite, grasshopper, moth, bee, butterfly, cricket, louse, ant, firefly, hornet, gnat, wasp, fly, cicada, aphid, flea, mayfly

ARACHNIDS—tick, black widow, scorpion, brown recluse, garden spider, tarantula, mite

CRUSTACEANS—lobster, barnacle, shrimp, crayfish, water flea, crab, wood louse

Page 7
Marine Life

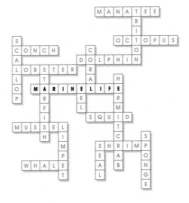

Page 8
Animals and the Environment
Recall
1. true
2. b
3. e
4. Food, shelter, and protection are three ways animals use their environment to live and survive.
5. Venn diagrams will vary.

Page 9
Metamorphosis
A. complete
1. egg
2. larva
3. pupa
4. adult
B. Incomplete
1. egg
2. nymph
3. adult

Page 10
Your Body Systems
skeletal, muscular nervous, sensory, endocrine digestive, respiratory, circulatory, urinary

Page 11
Your Hands and Feet

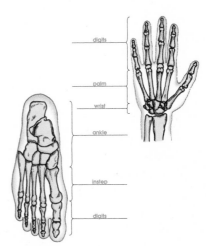

Page 12
Four Kinds of Teeth

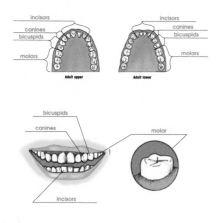

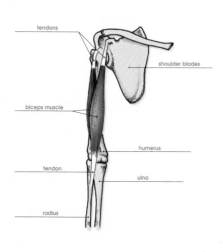

Page 13
Inside Your Teeth

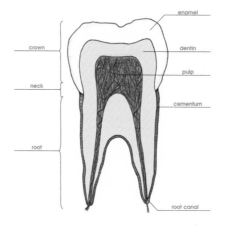

Page 14
Your Muscles

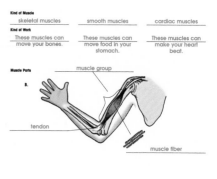

Page 15
Skeletal Muscles

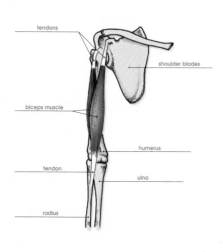

Page 16
Veins and Arteries

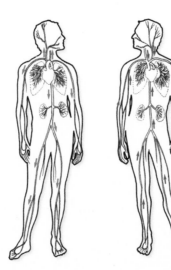

Page 17
Your Heart

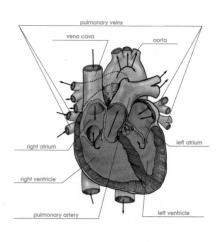

Page 18
Transmitters of Impulses

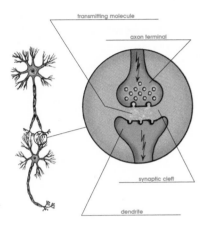

Page 19
Nervous System at Work

1. b
2. a
3. d
4. e
5. c

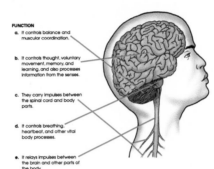

Page 20
Autonomic Nervous System

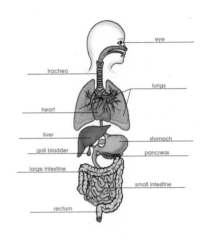

Page 21
Nervous System Review

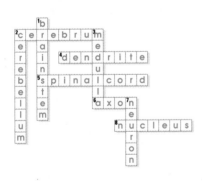

Page 22
Glands at Work

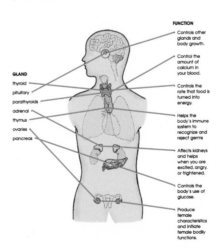

Page 23
The Sensory Systems

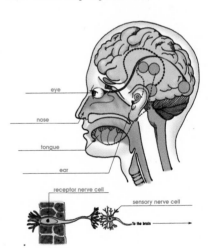

Page 25
Your Ear

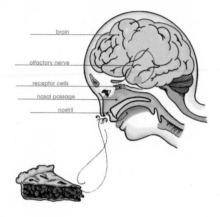

Page 26
Your Nose

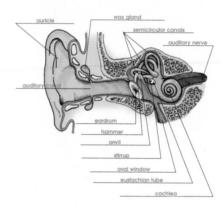

Page 27
Your Eye

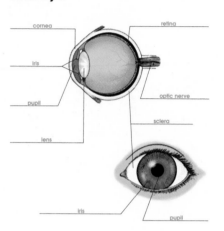

Page 28
Ear and Eye Review

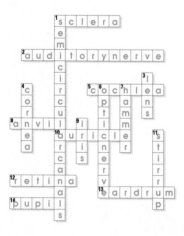

Page 29
Human Body Review

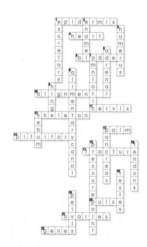

Page 30
Organ Systems

ORGANS	Digestive	Respiratory	Urinary	Reproductive	Circulatory	Nervous	Endocrine
Bladder			X				
Brain						X	
Heart					X		
Ovaries				X			X
Liver	X						
Pancreas	X						X
Kidney			X				
Spinal Cord						X	
Lungs		X					
Small Intestines	X						
Diaphragm		X					
Mouth	X	X					
Nerves						X	
Testes				X			X
Thyroid Gland							X
Arteries					X		
Esophagus	X						
Cerebellum						X	

Answer Key

Page 31
Inherited Traits
1. C
2. U
3. C
4. U
5. Paragraphs will vary.
6. Answers will vary.

Page 32
Beyond the Looking Glass
1. the basic unit of a living thing that performs all of the functions of life
2. an inherited unit of genetic material that determines a trait
3. Answers will vary.
4. at least 2; one from each parent
5. brown eyes are carried by a dominant gene
6. curly hair, because it is a dominant trait

Page 33
A Special Science Tool
a. nosepiece
b. coarse adjustment
c. fine adjustment
d. arm
e. base
f. eyepiece
g. body tube
h. objective
i. stage
j. diaphragm
k. stage clips
l. mirror

Page 37
Definitely Cellular
1. where proteins are made
2. jelly-like substance within the cell; holds other cell parts
3. chromosomes are found here; controls the activity of the rest of the cell parts
4. holds the nucleus together
5. releases energy from the nutrients
6. controls entry into and out of the cell
7. stores and releases chemicals
8. contains water and dissolved minerals

1. cell membrane
2. chloroplast

Page 38
Animal or Plant?

CHARACTERISTIC	PLANT	ANIMAL
Living organisms	✓	✓
Formed from cells	✓	✓
Cells have chlorophyll	✓	
Makes its own food	✓	
Gets food from outside		✓
Moves from place to place		✓
Has limited movement	✓	
Can reproduce its own kind	✓	✓
Depends on sun's energy	✓	✓

Page 41
Look Closer
1. Consumers—organisms that eat
2. Producers—all green plants
3. Sun—provides energy for everything on earth
4. Pesticides—chemicals used to eliminate pests such as bugs
5. Food chain—a system, like a chain, by which organisms get their food
6. Food web—food chains interwoven together
7. Domino effect—When one organism in a food chain is affected, other organisms in the chain and in the food web are impacted as well.
8. Energy—element necessary for life

1. domino effect
2. Answers will vary.

Page 43
You Are What You Eat

	CORN BALLS	YOUR CEREAL
What kind of grain(s) is used?	corn	Answers will vary.
Is sugar used?	yes	
What position is sugar on the list of ingredients?	2nd	
List other sweeteners.	corn syrup molasses	
How many calories per serving without milk?	110	
How many calories per serving when eaten with 1/2 cup of skim milk?	150	
How much protein per serving?	1 g	
How many vitamins and minerals does the cereal contain?	10	
How much cholesterol is in one serving?	0 mg	
How much fat is in one serving?	0 g	
How much carbohydrate is in one serving?	26 g	

Page 44
Enlightening Information
1. abiotic: sun, sky, water, rock biotic: butterfly, dragonfly, fish, turtle, cattails, snails, frogs, bugs
2. The living things in the picture depend on each other for food.
3. pond
4. Circle all the living things—plants and animals.
5. Frogs eat insects; insects eat plants; plants grow in water; fish live in water; etc.
6. frogs, fish, turtles, dragonflies, butterflies, etc.

Page 45
It's a Small World
1. plants and animals
2. based on their physical structures and behaviors
3. they all contain living things; their size
4. food, water, temperature, and minerals
5. a species must move to another habitat or die out

Page 47
Habitats Recall
1. b
2. a
3. true
4. c
5. a
Answers will vary.

Page 48
The Layered Look
1. inner core
2. outer core
3. mantle
4. crust
5. crust
6. Answers will vary.

Page 49
Bending the Earth's Crust

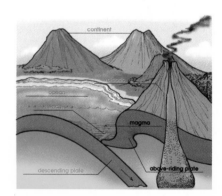

Page 50
Earth's Moving Plates

Page 51
U.S. Climate Zones
Answers will vary.
6-continental
1-alpine
1-alpine, 10-subarctic,
  3-tundra
7-subtropical, 2-steppe,
  5-desert
7-subtropical, 9-tropical
6-continental

Page 52
Cloud Words
1. feathery clouds
2. feathery, piled-up clouds
3. feathery clouds in sheets
(or stretched out)
4. high, piled-up clouds
5. high clouds in sheets (or
stretched out)
6. rain clouds in sheets (or
stretched out)
7. clouds in sheets (or layers
or stretched out)
8. piled-up clouds in sheets
(or stretched out)
9. piled-up clouds
10. piled-up rain clouds

Page 53
Name That Cloud
1. Cirrus
2. Cirrocumulus
3. Cirrostratus
4. Altocumulus
5. Altostratus
6. Nimbostratus
7. Stratus
8. Stratocumulus
9. Cumulus
10. Cumulonimbus

Page 54
A Magic Square of Weather
34; 4 squares in each corner
4 squares in center

mass of air that surrounds Earth	air that rushes in from the north and south to warm the air along the equator	calm areas of Earth where there is little wind	a gas in the upper part of Earth's atmosphere
1	15	14	4
cold air from the ocean that moves into the warmer land	the zone of the atmosphere above the troposphere	the zone of the atmosphere above the stratosphere	a movement of air close to Earth's surface
12	6	7	9
the outer zone of Earth's atmosphere	air above Earth that is warmed by the reflection of the sun's rays and is prevented from easily passing back into space	transfer of heat by currents of air or water	strong, steady winds high in the atmosphere; used by pilots
8	10	11	5
cold air from land that moves out to warmer air over oceans	zone of the atmosphere which affects the transmission of radio waves	the zone of the atmosphere which is closest to the surface of Earth	the line along which air masses meet
13	3	12	16

Page 55
Symbol Sense
A. 6
B. 10
C. 1
D. 16
E. 14
F. 2
G. 13
H. 4 (Symbols 5, 7, 12, and 15
are the "fakes")
I. 9
J. wrong label
K. 11
L. 8
M. 3
N. wrong label

77

Page 56
What's in a Name?
Before 1950
1860—Hurricane 1
The Great Hurricane of 1780
The Late Gale at St. Joseph
1950-1952
Hurricane King
Hurricane Easy
Hurricane Able
1952-1978
Hurricane Audrey
Hurricane Eloise
Hurricane Hazel
1978-Present
Hurricane Hugo
Hurricane George
Hurricane Mitch

Page 57
Defining Droughts
1. Definitions 5 and 6
2. Definition 1
3. Definition 4
4. Definition 3
5. Definition 2
6. Definition 1
7. Definitions 2, 4, and 6
8. Definition 5

Page 58
What Are You Wearing?
1. air temperature, air pressure, wind, humidity
2. shorts, T-shirt
3. barometer—air pressure anemometer—wind
4. Answers will vary.

Page 59
Earth and Moon
1. earth's diameter = 7,926 miles, moon's diameter = 2,160 miles
2. Answers will vary.
3. seasons

Page 60
Physical Characteristics of the Planets
Answers will vary.
1. The inner plants' distances are shorter.
2. It took longer.
3. because those planets are further away than Mercury
4. The year is longer the further away the planet is from the sun.

Page 61
Astronomical Alterations
2. quasar, D
3. pulsar, F
4. orbit, H
5. Mars, L
6. planet, A
7. moon, B
8. star, J
9. sun, E
10. comet, G
11. axis, I
12. meteor, C

ght Energy

12. T
13. T
14. T
5. T
. T
7. F
8. T
9. F
0. T
T
T

Page 63
The Behavior of Light
1. bent
2. reflected
3. light
4. real image
5. virtual
6. mirror
7. concave
8. retina
9. convex
10. focal
11. lens
12. index
13. image
14. photon
15. flat

Page 64
What Is Electricity?
1. battery
2. bulb
3. resistor
4. charge
5. electrode
6. circuit
7. insulator
8. conductor
9. switch
10. positive
11. negative
12. watt
13. ohm
14. fuse
15. ampere
16. generator
17. volt
18. turbine

om
d or attract
from or repel
ectrical energy
nature
ce of positive
charges

Page 66
How Many Volts?

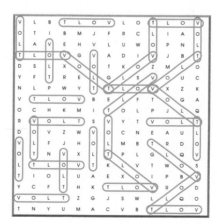

Page 67
Newton's Laws
Answers will vary.
1. 2
2. 1,3
3. 1,2,3
4. 1,3
5. 2

Page 68
Forms of Energy
1. potential
2. kinetic
3. kinetic
4. kinetic
5. potential
6. kinetic

Page 70
Six Types of Simple Machines
lever
inclined plane
screw
wedge
pulley
wheel and axle

Table of Contents
Advanced Concepts
Grade 4
Multiplication and Division • Word Problems • Statistics

Multiplication Fact Finder

Directions: Circle groups of numbers that make multiplication facts. Look horizontally and vertically.

4	1	9	3	27	0	3	1	1	8	9
4	1	1	1	0	9	7	63	0	7	1
16	2	3	5	4	20	21	0	1	56	9
0	2	0	7	6	42	1	7	7	49	1
8	4	32	1	1	8	3	24	0	4	0
1	0	3	3	9	1	0	5	1	9	0
8	1	0	6	5	30	1	6	6	36	4
1	0	5	0	45	4	7	28	2	4	8
42	8	8	64	1	0	5	7	35	1	9
6	1	40	1	7	7	5	1	0	1	2
8	9	72	5	3	15	25	0	6	3	18

Cobwebs

Directions: Write each missing factor. The product is on the outside ring. Color sections of each web with even numbers yellow. Color sections of each web with odd numbers green.

1.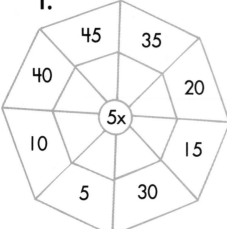

2.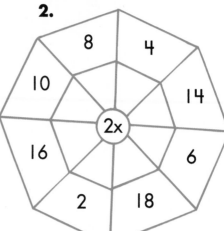

3.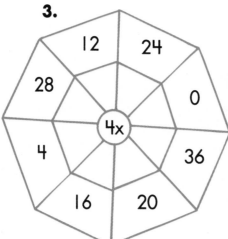

4.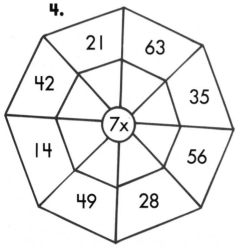

5.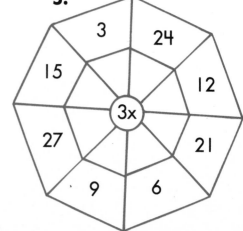

A New Team in Town

Did you know the Boston Bisons joined the Toledo Toucans to become a new NFL football team?

Directions: To find out what they are called now, solve each problem. Then, write the matching letter above the answer at the bottom of the page.

T 37 x 6	A 96 x 7	E 73 x 4	I 87 x 9	L 42 x 8
S 52 x 6	F 47 x 7	H 88 x 6	L 32 x 6	U 64 x 8
L 45 x 7	F 39 x 7	B 68 x 5	O 81 x 8	B 78 x 3

222 528 292   234 512 273 329 672 192 648

340 783 315 336 312

Name _____

Number Letters

Each problem has a letter in place of a number.

Directions: Use what you know about multiplication and division to determine the missing number.

1. $3 \times m = 12$

m = _____

2. $5 \times 8 = t$

t = _____

3. $b \times 7 = 42$

b = _____

4. $2 \times d = 4 \times 4$

d = _____

5. $45 = n \times 5$

n = _____

6. $6 \times 4 = a \times 8$

a = _____

7. $u \times 3 = 6 \times 5$

u = _____

8. $e = 7 \times 3$

e = _____

9. $24 = r \times 2$

r = _____

10. $4 \times t = 14 \times 2$

t = _____

11. $10 \times 4 = s \times 8$

s = _____

12. $3 \times 6 = 9 \times o$

o = _____

13. $14 \times e = 2 \times 7$

e = _____

14. $l = 6 \times 3$

l = _____

15. $c = 9 \times 3$

c = _____

Directions: Use the letters from each problem above matched with the answers below to reveal a message.

$\overline{\hspace{1em}}_{5} \ \overline{\hspace{1em}}_{7} \ \overline{\hspace{1em}}_{1} \ \overline{\hspace{1em}}_{3} \ \overline{\hspace{1em}}_{13} \ \overline{\hspace{1em}}_{9} \qquad \overline{\hspace{1em}}_{14} \ \overline{\hspace{1em}}_{13} \ \overline{\hspace{1em}}_{10} \ \overline{\hspace{1em}}_{10} \ \overline{\hspace{1em}}_{13} \ \overline{\hspace{1em}}_{9} \ \overline{\hspace{1em}}_{11}$

$\overline{\hspace{1em}}_{4} \ \overline{\hspace{1em}}_{12} \ \overline{\hspace{1em}}_{5} \ \overline{\hspace{1em}}_{10} \qquad \overline{\hspace{1em}}_{11} \ \overline{\hspace{1em}}_{15} \ \overline{\hspace{1em}}_{6} \ \overline{\hspace{1em}}_{9} \ \overline{\hspace{1em}}_{13} \qquad \overline{\hspace{1em}}_{1} \ \overline{\hspace{1em}}_{13}!$

6

Add Them Up

Multiplication is repeated addition.	
Example: 356	356
x 3	356
	+ 356
	1,068

Directions: Rewrite each multiplication problem as an addition problem. Solve.

1. 576
  x 4

2. 384
  x 2

3. 907
  x 3

4. 232
  x 6

5. 843
  x 4

6. 728
  x 3

7. 912
  x 5

8. 569
  x 2

9. 206
  x 7

10. 374
  x 6

Think: With what type of problems would you find this strategy helpful?

Multiplication

Multiply 32 x 23.

Step A	Step B	Step A	Step B
32 x 2 64	32 x 20 640	32 x 23 96	32 x 23 96 640

since   then

2 x 32 = _____   20 x 32 = _____

3 x 32 = _____   20 x 32 = _____

Step C   640 + 96 = _____

Directions: Multiply.

	a.	b.	c.	d.	e.	f.	g.
1.	14 x 20	22 x 40	23 x 30	51 x 50	33 x 20	71 x 60	71 x 80
2.	32 x 40	21 x 30	41 x 70	51 x 70	31 x 90	31 x 60	61 x 50
3.	13 x 12	12 x 31	21 x 34	23 x 21	31 x 33	14 x 22	21 x 14
4.	23 x 23	21 x 44	42 x 12	21 x 13	11 x 41	22 x 24	33 x 32

Multiplying by a Two-Digit Number

With Regrouping

1. Multiply by the ones.
8 x 7 = 56 (Carry the 5.)

5
67
x 38
6

Directions: Multiply.

37
x 24

77
x 21

2. Multiply by the ones.
8 x 6 = 48 + 5 = 53
(When they are completed,
cross out all carried digits.)

X̶
67
x 38
536

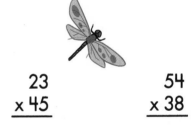

23
x 45

54
x 38

3. Multiply by the tens. Place
a zero in the ones column.
3 x 7 = 21 (Carry the 2.)

2X̶
67
x 38
536
10

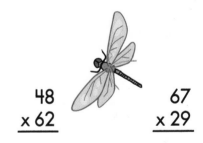

48
x 62

67
x 29

4. Multiply by the tens.
3 x 6 = 18 + 2 = 20

X̶X̶
67
x 38
536
2010

5. Add.
536 + 2010 = 2,546

X̶X̶
67
x 38
536
+2010
2,546

Now, check your answers
with a calculator.

Multiplication Practice

Directions: Multiply.

	a.	**b.**	**c.**	**d.**	**e.**
1.	89 x 21	58 x 92	97 x 53	63 x 80	76 x 10
2.	68 x 30	57 x 44	52 x 60	53 x 75	49 x 26
3.	74 x 50	74 x 89	62 x 97	69 x 40	54 x 38
4.	54 x 61	86 x 20	37 x 72	32 x 13	83 x 34
5.	43 x 66	85 x 88	65 x 55	54 x 78	38 x 47

Multiplication Drill

Directions: Multiply. Color the picture below by matching each number with its paintbrush.

| 134 | 48 | 876 | 432 |
| x 22 | x 66 | x 13 | x 64 |

| 68 | 5,478 | 248 | 6,897 |
| x 11 | x 8 | x 61 | x 6 |

| 82 | 6,798 | 79 | 694 |
| x 4 | x 5 | x 86 | x 38 |

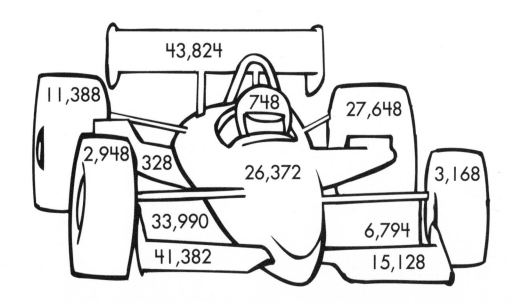

Up, Up, and Away

Directions: Multiply. Put the letters of the answers on the lines below to find out a secret message.

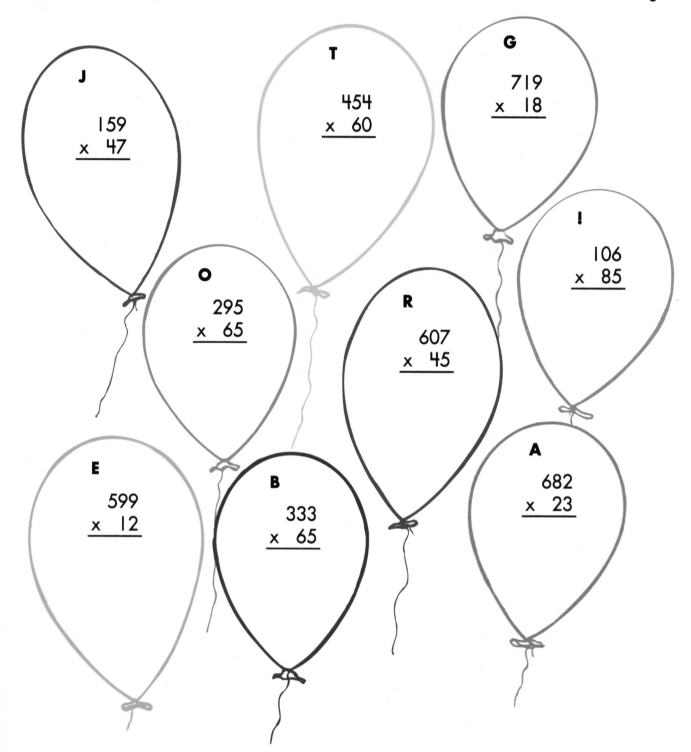

J
159
x 47

T
454
x 60

G
719
x 18

!
106
x 85

O
295
x 65

R
607
x 45

E
599
x 12

B
333
x 65

A
682
x 23

$\overline{\text{12,942}}$ $\overline{\text{27,315}}$ $\overline{\text{7,188}}$ $\overline{\text{15,686}}$ $\overline{\text{27,240}}$ $\overline{\text{7,473}}$ $\overline{\text{19,175}}$ $\overline{\text{21,645}}$ $\overline{\text{9,010}}$

Multiplication With Three Numbers

Multiply 538 x 426.

Step A	**Step B**	**Step C**	**Step D**
538	538	538	538
x 426	x 426	x 426	x 426
3228	3228	3228	3228
	10760	10760	10760
		215200	215200
			229,188

6 x 538 = 3,228

20 x 538 = 10,760

400 x 538 = 215,200

_____ + _____ + _____ = 229,188

Directions: Multiply.

	a.	**b.**	**c.**	**d.**	**e.**
1.	294	397	215	852	415
	x 473	x 245	x 169	x 386	x 352
2.	862	254	693	782	763
	x 792	x 577	x 968	x 848	x 635

What Exactly Is Division?

In division, you begin with an amount of something (the dividend), separate it into small groups (the divisor), then find out how many groups are created (the quotient).

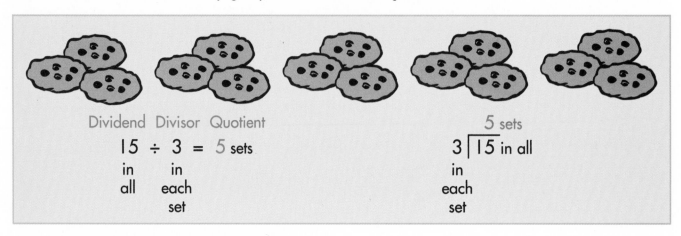

Directions: Solve these division problems.

$21 \div 3 =$ _____ $3\overline{)21}$ $18 \div 3 =$ _____ $3\overline{)18}$

$20 \div 5 =$ _____ $5\overline{)20}$ $16 \div 4 =$ _____ $4\overline{)16}$

$14 \div 7 =$ _____ $7\overline{)14}$ $12 \div 2 =$ _____ $2\overline{)12}$

$18 \div 2 =$ _____ $2\overline{)18}$ $24 \div 6 =$ _____ $6\overline{)24}$

A Rule to Live By

Name _____

T $9\overline{)9}$	A $6\overline{)30}$	T $2\overline{)2}$	
F $9\overline{)81}$	R $8\overline{)56}$	E $9\overline{)18}$	H $7\overline{)42}$
A $7\overline{)35}$	F $3\overline{)27}$	R $9\overline{)63}$	C $9\overline{)36}$
E $8\overline{)16}$	K $6\overline{)48}$	E $7\overline{)14}$	O $8\overline{)24}$
H $6\overline{)36}$	A $9\overline{)45}$	K $5\overline{)40}$	O $3\overline{)9}$
F $6\overline{)54}$	R $7\overline{)49}$	A $8\overline{)40}$	H $8\overline{)48}$

Directions: Write the letters on the lines to find a good rule to follow.

$\dfrac{T}{1}$ $\dfrac{\ }{5}$ $\dfrac{\ }{8}$ $\dfrac{\ }{2}$ $\dfrac{\ }{4}$ $\dfrac{\ }{5}$ $\dfrac{\ }{7}$ $\dfrac{\ }{2}$ $\dfrac{\ }{3}$ $\dfrac{\ }{9}$

$\dfrac{T}{1}$ $\dfrac{\ }{6}$ $\dfrac{\ }{2}$ $\dfrac{\ }{2}$ $\dfrac{\ }{5}$ $\dfrac{\ }{7}$ $\dfrac{T}{1}$ $\dfrac{\ }{6}$

Division

Name _____

Divide 4$\overline{)23}$.

Step A	**Step B**	**Step C**

$$\begin{array}{r} 5 \\ 4\overline{)23} \\ 20 \quad (5\times4) \end{array}$$

$$\begin{array}{r} 5 \\ 4\overline{)23} \\ 20 \\ \hline 3 \quad (23-20) \end{array}$$

$$\begin{array}{r} 5\ R3 \\ 4\overline{)23} \\ 20 \\ \hline 3 \quad \text{(remainder)} \end{array}$$

Directions: Divide.

	a.	b.	c.	d.	e.	f.	g.
1.	7 R2 6$\overline{)44}$ $\underline{42}$ 2	9$\overline{)38}$	3$\overline{)10}$	2$\overline{)15}$	8$\overline{)15}$	9$\overline{)47}$	7$\overline{)23}$
2.	4$\overline{)13}$	7$\overline{)15}$	6$\overline{)13}$	5$\overline{)24}$	6$\overline{)20}$	8$\overline{)20}$	5$\overline{)14}$
3.	8$\overline{)39}$	2$\overline{)19}$	9$\overline{)30}$	7$\overline{)32}$	3$\overline{)14}$	8$\overline{)34}$	4$\overline{)9}$
4.	6$\overline{)31}$	9$\overline{)12}$	6$\overline{)26}$	2$\overline{)17}$	9$\overline{)19}$	5$\overline{)31}$	2$\overline{)11}$
5.	8$\overline{)46}$	7$\overline{)41}$	4$\overline{)21}$	3$\overline{)16}$	4$\overline{)25}$	5$\overline{)22}$	3$\overline{)19}$

Division Drill

Name _____

Divide 7 ⟌ 949.

Step A	Step B	Step C

Step A

```
    1
7 ⟌ 949
    7    (1x7)
    2    (9–7)
```

Step B

```
    13
7 ⟌ 949
    7↓
    24
    21   (3x7)
     3   (24–21)
```

Step C

```
    135 R4
7 ⟌ 949
    7
    24
    21
    39
    35   (5x7)
     4   ( remainder)
```

Directions: Divide.

	a.	b.	c.	d.	e.
1.	3⟌563	5⟌682	9⟌955	8⟌939	2⟌675
2.	4⟌844	7⟌962	4⟌527	8⟌864	6⟌749
3.	4⟌647	6⟌822	3⟌559	7⟌976	5⟌780

Table Tool

Directions: Fill in the multiplication table to the right.

x	1	2	3	4	5	6	7	8	9
1									
2									
3									
4									
5									
6									
7									
8									
9									

Directions: Solve the division problems to find the quotients. Use the multiplication table to check your answers.

1. $28 \div 7 =$ _____   **2.** $36 \div 6 =$ _____   **3.** $63 \div 7 =$ _____

4. $20 \div 5 =$ _____   **5.** $24 \div 4 =$ _____   **6.** $8 \div 2 =$ _____

7. $81 \div 9 =$ _____   **8.** $6 \div 3 =$ _____   **9.** $54 \div 9 =$ _____

10. $48 \div 6 =$ _____   **11.** $7 \div 1 =$ _____   **12.** $27 \div 3 =$ _____

13. $56 \div 8 =$ _____   **14.** $9 \div 9 =$ _____   **15.** $54 \div 6 =$ _____

16. $16 \div 4 =$ _____   **17.** $10 \div 2 =$ _____   **18.** $64 \div 8 =$ _____

19. $36 \div 4 =$ _____   **20.** $4 \div 2 =$ _____   **21.** $35 \div 5 =$ _____

22. $5 \div 5 =$ _____   **23.** $49 \div 7 =$ _____   **24.** $12 \div 2 =$ _____

Jersey Division

Directions: Write the numbers in the correct footballs to get the given answer.

712

21 ÷ 7 = 3

423

◯ ÷ ◯ = 8

972

◯ ÷ ◯ = 3

848

◯ ÷ ◯ = 6

819

◯ ÷ ◯ = 2

554

◯ ÷ ◯ = 9

274

◯ ÷ ◯ = 6

658

◯ ÷ ◯ = 7

794

◯ ÷ ◯ = 7

376

◯ ÷ ◯ = 9

663

◯ ÷ ◯ = 6

804

◯ ÷ ◯ = 5

Round and Round

Directions: Divide. Then, use the code to solve the riddle.

A	N	K	M

1.

$$\begin{array}{r} 14\ R2 \\ 9\overline{)128} \\ -9 \\ \hline 38 \\ -36 \\ \hline 2 \end{array}$$

$$3\overline{)\$3.33}$$

$$9\overline{)487}$$

$$6\overline{)723}$$

U	S	R	T

2. $8\overline{)762}$ $7\overline{)4,280}$ $3\overline{)\$14.40}$ $9\overline{)643}$

P	E

3. $8\overline{)659}$ $5\overline{)\$15.95}$

Where would you find the world's biggest wheel?

A			A	
14 R2	71 R4		14 R2	$1.11

A								
14 R2	120 R3	95 R2	611 R3	$3.19	120 R3	$3.19	$1.11	71 R4

	A		
82 R3	14 R2	$4.80	54 R1

Doggie Trouble

Directions: Help the dog get to its bone by connecting the correctly done division problems to make a path.

85 R17 23⟌1972	30 R29 32⟌989	14 R27 43⟌629	232 R3 30⟌6963	107 R4 65⟌6959
104 R8 15⟌1508	31 R4 22⟌687	31 R12 19⟌582	78 R6 87⟌6933	155 R11 52⟌8071
255 R15 31⟌8013	14 R15 42⟌6231	20 R18 26⟌541	54 R9 18⟌819	31 R3 26⟌809
52 R27 60⟌3207	158 R31 39⟌6193	36 R11 27⟌983	115 R8 71⟌8203	58 R3 17⟌989
		18 R26 81⟌1484	44 R7 44⟌1943	63 R9 28⟌1773

21

Advanced Concepts: Grade 4

Wh-o-o-o Knows?

Directions: Find the quotients and the remainders.

1. $\overset{\text{8 R14}}{56\overline{)462}}$ $14\overline{)93}$ $44\overline{)249}$
        $\underline{-448}$
          14

2. $36\overline{)267}$ $41\overline{)352}$ $26\overline{)79}$ $53\overline{)245}$

3. $27\overline{)725}$ $44\overline{)673}$ $51\overline{)870}$ $39\overline{)497}$

4. $32\overline{)680}$ $17\overline{)473}$ $65\overline{)800}$ $13\overline{)277}$

Hmmm, What Should I Do?

Example: 52 $\left(+\right)$ 9 = 61

8 $\left(\times\right)$ 4 = 32

Directions: Write the correct symbols in the circles.

7 $\bigcirc$ 8 = 56   81 $\bigcirc$ 6 = 75   55 $\bigcirc$ 3 = 52

54 $\bigcirc$ 9 = 6   2 $\bigcirc$ 1 = 2   40 $\bigcirc$ 2 = 38

36 $\bigcirc$ 5 = 31   0 $\bigcirc$ 2 = 2   8 $\bigcirc$ 8 = 64

12 $\bigcirc$ 6 = 18   9 $\bigcirc$ 8 = 72   18 $\bigcirc$ 5 = 23

72 $\bigcirc$ 7 = 65   32 $\bigcirc$ 5 = 37

0 $\bigcirc$ 1 = 0   48 $\bigcirc$ 6 = 8

9 $\bigcirc$ 1 = 9   32 $\bigcirc$ 4 = 8

45 $\bigcirc$ 9 = 5   6 $\bigcirc$ 7 = 42

Balloon Bazaar

Directions: Multiply or divide to solve each problem.

$8.28 per dozen
Find the cost of 1.

$0.28 each
Find the cost of 30.

$0.15 each
Find the cost of 47.

$0.15
x   47
105
600
$7.05

$7.92 for 22
Find the cost of 1.

$1.89 each
Find the cost of 15.

$5.04 per dozen
Find the cost of 1.

$2.85 for 15
Find the cost of 1.

$9.60 for 20
Find the cost of 1.

$0.97 each
Find the cost of 42.

$2.29 each
Find the cost of 13.

Number Puzzles

Directions: Solve these number puzzles.

1

Write your age. _____

Multiply it by 3. _____

Add 18. _____

Multiply by 2. _____

Subtract 36. _____

Divide by 6. (your age) _____

2

Write any number. _____

Double that number. _____

Add 15. _____

Double again. _____

Subtract 30. _____

Divide by 2. _____

Divide by 2 again. _____

3

Write any 2-digit number. _____

Double that number. _____

Add 43. _____

Subtract 18. _____

Add 11. _____

Divide by 2. _____

Subtract 18. _____

4

Write the number of children in your neighborhood. _____

Double that number. _____

Add 15. _____

Double it again. _____

Subtract 30. _____

Divide by 4. _____

Mary Anning

Directions: Solve the problems.

1. 21 ÷ 7 = _____   peppers

2. 6 x 4 = _____   a

3. 3 x 4 = _____   of

4. 72 ÷ 8 = _____   peck

5. 14 ÷ 7 = _____   Mary

6. 36 ÷ 6 = _____   by

7. 7 x 7 = _____   picked

8. 56 ÷ 8 = _____   the

9. 3 x 5 = _____   pickled

10. 6 ÷ _____ = 6   seashore

11. 18 ÷ 2 = _____   lamb

12. 6 x _____ = 30   she

13. 2 x 4 = _____   seashells

14. 36 ÷ 9 = _____   sells

15. 4 x 5 = _____   Piper

16. 7 x 4 = _____   had

17. 6 x 6 = _____   Peter

18. _____ ÷ 8 = 4   little

Directions: Now, solve the following. Circle the tens digit in each answer. Locate the answers above that match the tens digits below. Write the matching words below each problem to find out what tongue twister was inspired by a girl named Mary Anning.

19. 467	20. 601	21. 942	22. 185	23. 526	24. 374
+ 289	− 453	− 553	+ 376	− 248	+ 236

_____ _____ _____ _____ _____ _____

Comparisons

Name_____

Directions: Circle the symbol that makes the statement true.

1. $14 + 22$ **< > =** $20 + 11$

2. $48 \div 4$ **< > =** $6 + 7$

3. $(5 \times 5) + 25$ **< > =** $100 - 50$

4. $77 + 20 - 6$ **< > =** $33 + 33 + 33$

Directions: Use at least two numbers and an operation to complete the statements below.

5. 9×8 **<** _____

6. $72 - 34$ **>** _____

7. $18 \div 96$ **>** _____

8. $231 + 57$ **=** _____

Directions: Replace each shape with a number to make the statements true.

9. ■ $- 8$ **<** 10

■ = _____

10. $26 +$ ▲ $= 73$

▲ = _____

11. $12 \div 6$ **>** ⬡

⬡ = _____

12. ⬤ $\times 3$ **<** 9

⬤ = _____

Explaining

Look at problems 9–12. Which problems will have more than one solution? Why?

Add and Subtract Story Problems

Directions: Find the answers. Show your work.

1. There were 509 people at the basketball game.
One hundred of those people were children.
How many of the people were not children?   _____

2. Allen counted 45 boys and 33 girls
on the school bus.
How many children were on the bus?   _____

How many more boys were on the bus?   _____

3. Marta counted 988 jelly beans.
Sixty-one jelly beans were yellow.
How many were not yellow?   _____

4. Juan's school meeting room can hold 382 people.
There are 252 people in the room.
How many more people can it hold?   _____

5. Amy and Kathy went bowling.
Amy had 212 points. Kathy had 255 points.
How many points did they have altogether?   _____

How many more points did Kathy have?   _____

6. Jenny bought 146 gum balls.
She gave some to her sister.
She had 102 gum balls left.
How many gum balls did she give to her sister?   _____

Wordy Problems

Directions: Solve each problem.

1. On Saturday, 709 people attended a football game. On Sunday, 983 people attended.

How many more people attended on Sunday? _____

How many people attended on Saturday and Sunday? _____

2. Barry and Jan were counting stars. Barry counted 179. Jan counted 184.

How many more did Jan count? _____

How many did they count altogether? _____

3. Jim bought a toy car for $11.50, a toy bike for $4.73, and $1.28 worth of candy.

How much money did Jim spend? _____

If he paid with $20.00, what was his change? _____

4. Mary went to the library to get books on animals and airplanes. The librarian said they had 4,228 books on animals and 3,119 books on airplanes.

How many more books did the library have on animals? _____

How many books were there on animals and airplanes? _____

5. While on vacation, Tasha picked out souvenirs for her friends back home. She picked out a hat for $8.26, a T-shirt for $12.79, and a sweatshirt for $17.35.

How much money did Tasha spend on her friends? _____

How much more did Tasha spend on the sweatshirt than on the hat? _____

6. The students at Hall Elementary School were competing in a read-a-thon with nearby Johnson Elementary. The students at Hall read 13,986 pages. The students at Johnson read 27,703 pages.

How many more pages did the students at Johnson Elementary read? _____

How many total pages did the students at both schools read? _____

If the fourth graders at Johnson Elementary read 5,672 pages, how many pages did the other students at Johnson read? _____

Par for the Course

Directions: Solve these problems by writing an equation. Remember to label your answer. (You may use a calculator and the information below to help.)

1. At Twin Lakes Golf Course, hole 1 is 230 ft. long, hole 2 is 185 ft. long, and the bridge across the lake is 8 ft. long. What is the total distance from hole 1 to hole 4?

_____

2. Jonah's drive off the second tee went 10 feet past the bridge. How far did Jonah drive his golf ball?

_____

3. The bridge is located between hole 3 and 4. If you cross the bridge twice during the first 4 holes, what is the total distance covered for the 4 holes?

_____

4. Andrew's ball rolled 27 feet past hole 6. How far did the ball travel?

_____

5. On hole 7, Sierra's ball traveled 190 feet and rolled 8 feet back from the hole. How far did her ball travel?

_____

6. Using the information on the chart, how long is the golf course?

_____

Twin Lakes	
Hole	**Distance**
1	230 ft.
2	185
3	201
4	143
5	248
6	120
7	193
8	200
9	130
Total length	

Wacky Waldo's Snow Show

Wacky Waldo's Snow Show is an exciting and fantastic sight. Waldo has trained whales and bears to skate together on the ice. There is a hockey game between a team of sharks and a pack of wolves. Elephants ride sleds down steep hills. Horses and buffaloes ski swiftly down mountains.

Directions: Write each problem and its answer.

1. Wacky Waldo has 4 ice-skating whales. He has 4 times as many bears who ice skate. How many bears can ice skate? _____ x _____ = _____	**4.** The Wolves' hockey team has 4 gray wolves. It has 8 times as many red wolves. How many red wolves does it have? _____ x _____ = _____
2. Waldo's Snow Show has 4 shows on Thursday, but it has 6 times as many on Saturday. How many shows are there on Saturday? _____ x _____ = _____	**5.** Waldo taught 6 buffaloes to ski. He was able to teach 5 times as many horses to ski. How many horses did he teach? _____ x _____ = _____
3. The Sharks' hockey team has 3 great white sharks. It has 6 times as many tiger sharks. How many tiger sharks does it have? _____ x _____ = _____	**6.** Buff, a skiing buffalo, took 7 nasty spills when he was learning to ski. His friend Harry Horse fell down 8 times as often. How many times did Harry fall? _____ x _____ = _____

Multiplying With Molly

Directions: Write the problem and the answer for each question.

1. Molly is the toughest football player in her school. She ran for 23 yards on one play and went 3 times as far on the next play. How far did she run the second time?

4. Molly stuffed 3 sticks of gum in her mouth in the morning. In the afternoon, she crammed 9 times as many sticks into her mouth. How many sticks did she have in the afternoon?

2. Molly keeps a rock collection. She has 31 rocks in one sack. She has 7 times as many under her bed. How many rocks are under her bed?

5. Molly did 51 multiplication problems in math last week. This week, she did 8 times as many. How many did she do this week?

3. Molly had 42 marbles when she came to school. She went home with 4 times as many. How many did she go home with?

6. Molly did 21 science experiments last year. This year, she did 7 times as many. How many experiments did she do this year?

32

Step by Step

Name _____

Directions: Read the problems below. Write each answer in the space provided.

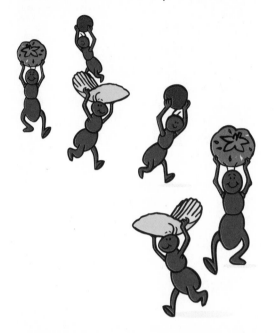

1. One battalion of ants marches with 25 ants in a row. There are 35 rows of ants in each battalion. How many ants are in one battalion?

_____

2. The Ant Army finds a picnic! Now, they need to figure out how many ants should carry each piece of food. A team of 137 ants moves a celery stick. They need 150 ants to carry a carrot stick. A troop of 121 ants carries a very large radish. How many ants in all are needed to move the vegetables?

_____

Work Space

3. Now, the real work begins—the big pieces of food that would feed their whole colony. It takes 1,259 ants to haul a peanut butter and jelly sandwich. It takes a whole battalion of 2,067 ants to lug the lemonade back, and it takes 1,099 ants to steal the pickle jar. How many soldiers carry these big items?

_____

4. Lookouts are posted all around the picnic blanket. It takes 53 soldiers to watch in front of the picnic basket. Another group of 69 ants watch out by the grill. Three groups of 77 watch the different trails in the park. How many ant-soldiers are on the lookout?

_____

Bargain Bonanza at Pat's Pet Place

Directions: Pat is having a gigantic sale. Help him divide his animals into groups for the sale.

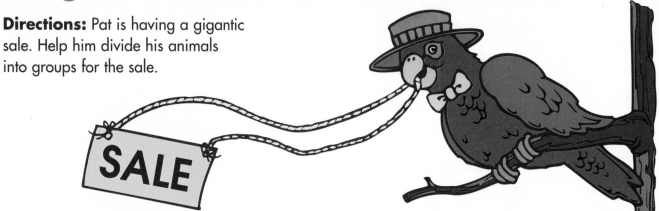

1. Pat has 84 rabbits. He is putting 4 rabbits in each cage. How many cages does he need?	**4.** Pat has 324 goldfish. If he puts 6 goldfish in each bag, how many plastic bags will he need?
2. Pat sells guppies in plastic bags with 5 guppies in each bag. He has 195 guppies. How many plastic bags does he need?	**5.** Pat received 116 hamsters. He keeps them in cages of 4 each. How many cages does he need for his hamsters?
3. Pat has 392 white mice. They are kept in cages of 7 mice each. How many cages does Pat need?	**6.** Pat has 120 parrots. They live in bird cages with 3 to each cage. How many bird cages does Pat need?

Humpback Whales

Directions: Solve the following word problems.

1. One humpback whale can eat 4,400 popcorn-size krill in
1 meal. How many krill are eaten if 8 whales have a meal?   _____

2. A humpback's flippers can be 17 feet long.
What is the total length of the 2 flippers?   _____

3. A humpback whale will migrate 5,000 miles one way
going from the summer feeding grounds to the winter
breeding grounds. How many miles will it make round trip?   _____

4. There are about 30,000 humpback whales alive today.
This is 30 times more than in 1965.
How many whales were alive in 1965?   _____

5. A humpback whale can measure 40 feet long.
How long would a group of 9 whales be end to end?   _____

6. Maddie likes the monthly magazine <u>Whales</u>.
A 1-year subscription is $16.32.
One copy at the store is $1.76.
How much would she save each month
if she purchased the subscription?   _____

How much would she save in 1 year?   _____

7. A humpback can weigh 40 tons. This is the same as
8 full-grown male African elephants. How much does
1 elephant weigh?   _____

Story Problems

Directions: Read the problems and solve by multiplying or dividing.

1. Mrs. Webb drives a total of 25 miles to and
from work each day. She works 5 days a week.
How many miles does she drive each week?   _____

2. The Produce Company sent Jack's Market 3 boxes of apples.
Each box weighed 83 pounds.
How much did the 3 boxes weigh?   _____

3. Mrs. Barry baked 24 cookies for her 4 children.
How many cookies did each child receive?   _____

4. David delivers 901 newspapers each week.
How many newspapers will he deliver in 9 weeks?   _____

5. Henry read 56 pages each day for three days.
How many pages did he read in 3 days?   _____

6. Karen and Barbara have 138 books to organize.
How many books will they each have if they
divide the books equally?   _____

7. The post office has 864 letters to deliver.
There are 8 mail carriers.
How many letters will each mail carrier deliver?   _____

8. Tammy practices piano for 55 minutes each day.
How many minutes does she practice in 65 days?   _____

9. Mr. Adams makes $8.25 each hour.
How much does he make in 8 hours?   _____

Which Problem Is Correct?

Name _____

Directions: Circle the equation on the left you should use to solve the problem. Then, solve the problem. Remember the decimal point in money questions. Add the dollar signs ($) to those answers.

1.
```
   56        56
 + 17       − 17
 ————       ————
```
Bill and his friends collect baseball cards. Bill has 17 fewer cards than Mack. Bill has 56 cards. How many baseball cards does Mack have?

2.
```
   54      3 ⟌ 54
 ×  3
 ————
```
Amos bought 54 baseball cards. He already had 3 times as many. How many baseball cards did Amos have before his latest purchase?

3.
```
   3.80      3.80
 + 3.50    − 3.50
 —————     —————
```
Joe paid $3.50 for a Mickey Mantle baseball card. Ted Williams cost him $3.80. How much more did he pay for Ted Williams than for Mickey Mantle?

4.
```
   3.60     9 ⟌ 3.60
 ×    9
 —————
```
Will bought 9 baseball cards for $3.60. How much did he pay per (for each) card?

5.
```
   8.00       8.00
 +  .50     −  .50
 —————      —————
```
Babe Ruth baseball cards were selling for $8.00. Herb Score baseball cards sold for 50 cents. Herb Score cards sold for how much less than Babe Ruth cards?

6.
```
   0.75      8 ⟌ 0.75
 ×    8
 —————
```
Andy bought 8 baseball cards at 75 cents each. How much did Andy pay in all?

Map Story Problems

Directions: Use this map of California to help you answer questions. Show your work on another sheet of paper.

California

San Francisco
414 miles

Sacramento
380 miles

Fresno
218 miles

Los Angeles

San Diego
124 miles

1. Jenny drove from Fresno to Los Angeles, then from Los Angeles to San Diego. How many miles did she drive altogether?

   _____

2. Starting from Los Angeles, how many more miles is it to San Francisco than to Sacramento?

   _____

3. It took Mr. Jones 2 hours to drive from San Diego to Los Angeles. How many miles did he drive each hour? _____

4. It took Mrs. Larson 4 days to drive from San Diego to Sacramento. How many miles did she drive? _____

   If she drove the same number of miles each day, how many miles did she drive each day? _____

5. Mr. and Mrs. Anderson took 2 days to drive from Los Angeles to San Francisco. If they drove the same number of miles each day, how many miles did they drive each day? _____

6. John and his family drove from San Francisco to San Diego. How many miles did they travel? _____

   How many miles did they travel going to San Diego and back home to San Francisco? _____

Perplexing Problems

Directions: Solve these problems.

Mark, David, Curt, and Jordan rented a motorized skateboard for 1 hour. What was the cost for each of them—split equally 4 ways? **Total:** $17.36 $_____	Five students pitched in to buy Mr. Foley a birthday gift. How much did each of them contribute? **Total:** $9.60 $_____

Mary, Cheryl, and Betty went to the skating rink. What was their individual cost? **Total:** $7.44 $_____	Carol, Katelyn, and Kimberly bought lunch at their favorite salad shop. What did each of them pay for lunch? **Total:** $12.63 $_____	Debbie, Sarah, Michele, and Kelly earned $6.56 altogether collecting cans. How much did each of them earn individually? **Total:** $6.56 $_____
Five friends went to the Hot Spot Café for lunch. They all ordered the special. What did it cost? **Total:** $27.45 $_____	Lee and Ricardo purchased an awesome model rocket together. What was the cost for each of them? **Total:** $9.52 $_____	The total fee for Erik, Bill, and Steve to enter the science museum was $8.76. What amount did each of them pay? **Total:** $8.76 $_____

A Day at the Ballpark

CONCESSION FOOD

Peanuts		$1.50
Popcorn		$1.25
Cola	small	$1.00
	medium	$1.75
	large	$2.25
Caramel corn		$2.00
Hot dog		$1.75
Candy bar		$1.00
Pizza		$2.50

TICKETS

	Adults	Children (under 12)
Box seats	$28.00	$12.00
Reserved	$18.00	$9.00
Bleachers	$8.00	$4.00

Directions: Solve the problems.

1. The Miller family, Mr. Miller, Mrs. Miller, 9-year-old Sarah, and 13-year-old David, went to the ballpark to cheer for their favorite team.

   How much would it cost if they sat in the box seats?   _____

   How much if they sat in the reserved seats?   _____

   How much if they sat in the bleachers?   _____

2. Dad wants to buy a hot dog, large cola, and a bag of peanuts. How much will it cost if there is no tax?   _____

3. Dad bought a pizza and a small cola for each person in the family. How much did he spend?   _____

4. Make up a "Day at the Ballpark" story problem of your own. Exchange it with a friend.

   _____

   _____

Too Much Information

Directions: Sometimes there is too much information. Cross out the information not needed and solve the problems.

4. Six of the students spent a total of $16.50 for refreshments and $21.00 for their tickets. How much did each spend for refreshments?

1. All 20 of the students from Sandy's class went to the movies. Tickets cost $3.50 each. Drinks cost $0.95 each. How much altogether did the students spend on tickets?

5. Of the students, 11 were girls and 9 were boys. At $1.50 per ticket, how much did the boys' tickets cost altogether?

2. Five students had ice cream, 12 others had candy. Ice cream cost $0.75 per cup. How much did the students spend on ice cream?

6. Mary paid $0.95 for an orange drink and $0.65 for a candy bar. Sarah paid $2.50 for popcorn. How much did Mary's refreshments cost her?

3. Seven of the 20 students did not like the movie. Three of the 20 students had seen the movie before. How many students had not seen the movie before?

7. Ten of the students went back to see the movie again the next day. Each student paid $3.50 for a ticket, $2.50 for popcorn, and $0.95 for a soft drink. How much did each student pay?

Money Matters

Directions: Find the answers.

1. Janet went to the store and bought meat for $2.20 and bread for eighty cents. How much did she spend at the store? _____

2. Amy had $4.30. She spent $1.99 on a game. How much did she have left? _____

3. Brad earned $5.00 mowing lawns. He spent $1.10 and saved the rest. How much did Brad save? _____

4. Cora earns $4.50 a week for babysitting. How much will she make in 4 weeks? _____

5. Twenty people each spent $5.98 for dinner. How much money did they spend altogether? _____

6. Mrs. Smith gave Jay $3.10 to spend at the fair. He returned with eleven cents. How much money did Jay spend at the fair? _____

7. Sammy saved $7.58 in March and $8.56 in April. How much did Sammy save in the two months? _____

   How much more did he save in April? _____

8. Martha makes $1.19 each day. How much did Martha make in 28 days? _____

9. Larry has $3.66. His older brother Scott has $6.56. How much do they have together? _____

   How much more does Scott have? _____

10. Roger earns $2.50 helping his dad at the store each day. How much will Roger have after 45 days? _____

42 *Advanced Concepts: Grade 4*

A 5-Step Formula

5-Step Formula	Step 1: What is the question?
	Step 2: What facts are important?
	Step 3: What information is not needed?
	Step 4: What operation (+, −, x, or ÷) should be used?
	Step 5: Use the operation and the important information to solve the problem.

Directions: Use the 5-step formula.

A squirrel can run 12 mph over a short distance. An elephant can run 25 mph. An ostrich can run 15 mph faster than an elephant. How fast can an ostrich run?

1. What question are you being asked to answer?

2. Underline the important information. Write that information here.

3. Cross out the information that is not needed.

4. What words in the problem help you decide which operation to use?

5. Solve the problem. Show your work.

Reflecting

You might need to read a problem more than once to complete the 5-step formula. What will be different about each time you read the problem?

Using the 5-Step Formula

Directions: Use the 5-step formula to answer each question.

1. Terron paints portraits of people and animals. He likes painting portraits of dogs best. The paint and other supplies cost $11 for each painting. He is going to paint 5 portraits. How much does he have to charge for each painting if he wants to make a $26 profit on each?

    a. What information is not necessary?

    b. Solve the problem. Show your work.

    c. What operation did you use (+, −, x, ÷) to find the answer?

    d. How did you know you were choosing the correct operation?

2. Juanita creates large murals. Her supplies cost $47.75 for each mural. She wants to earn a $25 profit on each mural. She spent $143.25 on supplies. How many murals did she buy supplies for? Show your work.

3. Bruce makes sculptures from wood, paper, glue, and paint. Each sculpture costs $21.98 for supplies. He wants to earn a $43.24 profit on each sculpture. How much will he spend on supplies if he wants to make 8 sculptures?

Expanding

Write your own math problem about an art project. Can it be solved using the 5-Step Formula? Why or why not?

Leftovers

> Sometimes you must think about the meaning of the **remainder** of a division problem. If the answer must be a whole number, then you must decide whether to round up or round down.

Directions: Solve the following story problems.

1. Chandra is storing her family's sweaters in boxes for the summer. She has 18 sweaters. Each box will hold 4 sweaters.

   a. How many boxes does she need?

   b. What did you do with the remainder? Why?

2. The Library Club has $525 for a summer picnic.

   a. They use half of the money for food. How much money will they have left over for entertainment, decorations, and prizes?

   b. What did you do with the remainder? Why?

3. The Library Club has $187 for prizes.

   a. How many $2 prizes could the club buy?

   b. How many $3 prizes could the club buy?

   c. What did you do with the remainder in each of these problems? Why?

4. There will be 152 people at the picnic. Six people can fit at each table.

   a. How many tables will be needed?

   b. What did you do with the remainder? Why?

Expanding

Write a problem using division that has a remainder. Explain what the remainder means. How does the remainder affect the answer?

Multiple-Step Problems

Directions: Some problems take more than one step to solve. You must decide how to solve each step, and in which order to solve them.

1. Over summer break, Melissa and Emmitt worked at the movie theater. Melissa worked 6 hours each day, 3 days a week. Emmitt worked twice as many hours a week as Melissa. The season lasted 14 weeks. How many hours did each of them work during the season?

a. How many hours did Melissa work each week? Show your work.

b. How many hours did Emmitt work each week? Show your work.

c. How many hours did Melissa work in the entire season? Show your work.

d. How many hours did Emmitt work for the entire season? Show your work.

2. On a school trip, 3 buses of students go to the museum. Each bus has 54 students. Each student spends $7 on admission. How much money do the students spend altogether?

a. How many students go to the museum? Show your work.

b. How much money do the students spend altogether? Show your work.

3. The Student Council is having a bake sale. The president brings 2 dozen sugar cookies. The vice president brings 3 dozen peanut-butter cookies. The secretary and treasurer each bring 60 chocolate-chip cookies. They are selling bags with 3 cookies each. How many bags of cookies do they have to sell? Show your work.

Reflecting

Look at problem 1. Could you have solved the problem by answering the questions in a different order? Could you have used different steps to solve the problem? Explain.

Smart Shopper

Directions: Solve the following story problems.

1. Theo goes shopping for cereal. The same cereal is available in 2 different sizes. A 16 oz. box costs $4.37. A 20 oz. box costs $5.22. Which would be the best buy?

   a. If 16 oz. cost $4.37, 1 oz. would cost $4.37 ÷ 16 = _____.

   b. If 20 oz. cost $5.22, 1 oz. would cost _____ = _____.

   c. The _____ oz. box would be the better buy.

2. Kiwadin could buy a 3 lb. bag of oranges for $1.69. There are a dozen oranges in the bag. He could buy oranges separately for $0.20 each. Should he buy the oranges separately, or in a bag? Explain.

3. Charles bought a box of 50 baseball cards for $25.00. His friend Deshawn likes to buy cards in packs of 10 for $4.00 each. Which boy got the better buy? Explain.

Explaining

How do you find the price per ounce if you know the price for 12 ounces?

Is That Exact?

If you do not need an exact answer, you should round the numbers and then **estimate**. If you need an **exact** answer, you must use the numbers given.

Directions: Circle **estimate** or **exact**. Then, calculate the estimate or exact amount.

1. Maya has 24 stamps from Canada, 11 stamps from Africa, and 72 stamps from the United States. Does Maya have more than 100 stamps?

   estimate   **exact**

2. On Thursday, 578 people came to the school play. On Friday, 634 people came. On Saturday, 919 people came. How many people came to the school play during the three days?

   estimate   **exact**

3. The Astronomy Club needs $550 to buy a new telescope. They earned $230 with a car wash, $190 with a bake sale, and $100 with a dog wash. Do they have enough money to buy the telescope?

   estimate   **exact**

4. Jay saved $100. He wants to buy presents for his family. For his dad, he finds a set of golf balls costing $24.50. He finds a $31.99 sweater for his mom. For his little sister, he wants a doll for $18.99. Will he have any money left over after these purchases?

   estimate   **exact**

Explaining

For what type of questions is an estimate appropriate?

Use Your Head

Directions: Estimate and solve the problem in your head.
Write your answer. Then, solve using paper and pencil.
You may use any strategies you are comfortable using.

1. Danielle has 3 quarters in her pocket. She has 5 dimes
in her backpack. She wants to buy a bag of chips and
a pop for $1.09. Does she have enough money?   _____

2. Emily bought a package of 72 pencils with holiday toppers.
She wants to give one to each person in her classroom, her
brother's classroom, and her sister's classroom. She has 26
students in her class, her brother has 24 students in his class,
and her sister has 25 students in her class. Does she have
enough pencils for every person?   _____

3. Miguel wants to purchase a binder for $3.52, a
pack of pencils for 84¢, and 6 folders for 24¢ each.
He has $5.00. Does he have enough money?   _____

4. Ramiro is collecting food package points. If he collects
475 points, he will have enough to order a computer game.
He collected 57 in June, 107 in July, 230 in August, and 61
in September. Does he have enough to place his order?   _____

5. Maria needs enough donuts for two classrooms of 26.
Donuts come in packages of 12. If she buys 4 packages,
does she have enough or need to buy one more?   _____

6. Brent needs 2,647 toothpicks to complete a sculpture.
He has an open box with 847 toothpicks in it. He found a
box at the store with 500 toothpicks in it. What is the smallest
number of boxes he needs to complete his project?   _____

Money Riddles

Directions: Read the riddles to determine the coins. Then, show how you know your answers are correct.

1. All 8 of my coins are silver in color.
Their total is 50¢.
What are they?

5. I have 7 coins worth $1.10.
I have no more than 3 of any coin.
What are my coins?

2. I have 36¢.
I have 1 each of 3 different coins.
What are my coins?

6. I have 5 coins worth 50¢.
I have at least 2 different types of coins.
What are the coins?

3. I have 5 coins worth 86¢.
None of the coins are nickels.
What are the coins?

7. I have 74¢.
I have 3 types of coins, but no nickels.
I have an even number of each coin.
What are the coins?

4. I have 2 different kinds of coins
worth 52¢. There are 12 coins total.
What are they?

8. I have 2 types of coins.
They equal 79¢.
What are the coins?

Explaining

Show 2 ways to make 68¢. Choose one way
and write a riddle for it.

Choose Your Operation

Directions: Read each problem. Circle the function you would use to solve it. Explain to a friend how you decided which operation to choose. Solve the problems.

+ − x ÷   **1.** The red bike costs $154.78. The blue bike costs $132.50. How much more does the red bike cost?

+ − x ÷   **2.** The administration wants to assign 2,082 students to 6 schools. How many students are in each school?

+ − x ÷   **3.** 15,860 beads were put into 65 bags. How many beads are in each bag?

+ − x ÷   **4.** Mike bought 4 new shirts. Each shirt cost $15.88. How much were the shirts before tax?

+ − x ÷   **5.** There are 345 students at Valley Elementary and 409 students at Hilltop Elementary. How many students attend both schools?

+ − x ÷   **6.** Jackie made a 74-minute long distance telephone call. Her mother charged her the 6¢ a minute from the phone bill. How much did Jackie owe her mother?

+ − x ÷   **7.** Tara reads 13 pages each night. How long does it take her to finish her 195-page book?

+ − x ÷   **8.** The container holds enough mix to make 18 servings of mashed potatoes. If each serving needs 3 scoops of mix, how many scoops of mix are in the container?

+ − x ÷   **9.** Matthew is required to practice his horn for 180 minutes a week. He has already practiced for 124 minutes. How many minutes does he still need to practice?

+ − x ÷   **10.** Jamal's family collects state quarters. They have 127 quarters in one container and 235 quarters in another container. How many quarters do they have altogether?

"Sum" Patterns

Name _____

Directions: Find a pattern in each row of numbers. Continue the pattern. Describe the pattern.

1. 1, 2, 3, 5, 8, 13, _____, _____, _____, _____, _____

2. 3, 5, 8, 13, 21, 34, _____, _____, _____, _____, _____

3. 1, 4, 5, 9, 14, 23, _____, _____, _____, _____, _____

4. 1, 3, 4, 7, 11, 18, _____, _____, _____, _____, _____

5. 2, 4, 6, 10, 16, 26, _____, _____, _____, _____, _____

Reflecting

What do each of these patterns have in common? Are they growing or decreasing patterns? How do they change? Why do you think this page is called "Sum" Patterns?

Adding and Subtracting Patterns

If a pattern has a **steady rate**, it changes by the same amount each time.

Directions: Finish the number patterns. Describe each pattern.

1. 55 52 49 46 _____ _____ _____ _____

2. 16 23 30 37 _____ _____ _____ _____

3. 115 100 85 70 _____ _____ _____ _____

4. 50 149 248 347 _____ _____ _____ _____

5. Which of the patterns are **growing patterns**? How do you know?

6. Which of the patterns are **decreasing patterns**? How do you know?

7. How does each of these patterns change?

Expanding

Write a pattern of your own. Describe your pattern. Compare your pattern with other patterns on this page. How is it the same? How is it different?

Number Patterns

Directions: Solve these number pattern problems.

1. Look at the number pattern.

| 1 | 2 | 4 | 7 | 11 | 16 | 22 |

+1   + 2

a. Is this a **growing pattern** or a **decreasing pattern**? _____

b. Does this pattern change at a **steady rate**? _____

c. Write the amount of change below each pair of numbers. The first two pairs have been done for you.

d. Describe the pattern from one number to the next.

2. Find the pattern. Fill in the missing numbers.

52 43 35 28 22 _____ _____ _____ _____

a. How is this pattern different from the pattern in problem 1?

b. How is this pattern similar to the pattern in problem 1?

c. Describe the pattern from one number to the next.

3. Look at the number pattern.

33   25   19   15   13

– 8   – 6

a. Is this a **growing pattern** or a **decreasing pattern**? _____

b. Write the amount of change below each pair of numbers. The first two pairs have been done for you.

c. Describe the pattern in the amount of change from one number to the next.

Number Patterns (cont.)

Directions: Find the pattern. Fill in the missing numbers. Describe each pattern.

4. 78 67 58 51 _____ _____ _____

5. 4 7 13 22 34 _____ _____ _____

6. 7 9 13 19 _____ _____ _____

7. Write this growing pattern as a decreasing pattern. Describe the pattern.

   36   39   43   48   54   61

8. Write this decreasing pattern as a growing pattern. Describe the pattern.

   68   64   58   50   40   28

Comparing

Compare growing patterns and decreasing patterns.
Explain how to examine a pattern to determine its type.

Let's Compare

Directions: Write **>** for greater than or **<** for less than.

1. 10,769 ◯ 11,200   177,204 ◯ 116,791   97,213 ◯ 107,213

2. 86,190 ◯ 84,993   981,203 ◯ 918,203   72,218 ◯ 75,003

3. 198,221 ◯ 98,221   264,193 ◯ 266,001   83,103 ◯ 80,793

4. 656,183 ◯ 665,183   199,820 ◯ 198,993   55,186 ◯ 54,939

5. Write the numbers in order on the chart below.

| 756,802 | 694,213 | 820,000 | 971,246 | 378,461 | 192,874 |
| 471,622 | 216,606 | 92,813 | 87,214 | 63,744 | 55,806 |

Big	Bigger	Biggest
1.	5.	9.
2.	6.	10.
3.	7.	11.
4.	8.	12.

6. The smallest number is _____.

   The largest number is _____.

7. Write the number that is 10 less than the smallest number. _____

   Write the number that is 100 more than the smallest number. _____

   Write the number that is 1,000 more than the largest number. _____

Name _____

You're the Greatest!

Directions: Compare each pair of numbers. Write **<** or **>** in each ◯.

1. 5,361 ⊙> 5,300

2. 9,327 ◯ 9,237

3. 10,561 ◯ 10,651

4. 593,461 ◯ 593,614

5. 98,997 ◯ 100,016

6. 497,843 ◯ 496,912

7. 600,000 ◯ 600,010

8. 1,493,017 ◯ 1,947,413

9. 31,113,311 ◯ 13,331,113

10. 1,087,789 ◯ 987,911

11. 235,400 ◯ 234,900

12. 893,982 ◯ 892,983

13. 203,960 ◯ 230,141

14. 156,651 ◯ 651,156

15. 93,825 ◯ 94,053

16. 23,985,310 ◯ 29,385,013

17. 19,675,902 ◯ 20,001,000

18. 63,814,910 ◯ 59,950,418

Directions: Arrange the numbers in each group from the least to the greatest.

1. 59,359; 590,359; 509,359; 95,359

_____

2. 417,003; 950,398; 409,985; 398,051

_____

3. 24,890; 20,561; 24,279; 24,385

_____

4. 831,485; 813,485; 89,497; 830,549

_____

On the Average . . .

An **average** is found by adding numbers and dividing them by the total number of addends. See the example in the box.

The children on the 6-on-6 basketball team made the following number of baskets:

April	1	Beth	3
Colton	3	Ryan	1
Jen	2	J.J.	2

The school paper wants to write about the game, but they don't have room for such a long list. Instead, the reporter will find the **average** by following the steps below.

Steps

1. **Add** all the team members' baskets together.

   _____ + _____ + _____ + _____ + _____ + _____ = _____

2. **Count** to find out how many team members there were.

   _____

3. **Divide** your answer for step 1 by the number in step 2.

   _____ ÷ _____ = _____

The paper will report that each team member normally makes an average of 2 baskets each.
Remember: add, count, divide.

Directions: Find the average for the following problem:
In their last 3 games, the Longlegs scored 24 points, 16 points, and 20 points.

1. Add.   2. Count.   3. Divide.

What was their average? _____.

58

Odd and Even Tug of War

Directions: Find the average for each group of numbers. Circle the averages.

1. 12, 35, 34, 15 12 $\overset{\textstyle ⟨24⟩}{4\overline{)96}}$ 35 − 8 34 16 +15 − 16 96 0	**2.** 39, 44, 84, 33	**3.** 121, 116, 132
4. 36, 10, 33, 45	**5.** 4, 5, 4, 9, 8	**6.** 214, 376, 148
7. 21, 36, 14, 13	**8.** 137, 275, 215	**9.** 62, 41, 77

How many averages were odd? _____

How many averages were even? _____

Which team won the tug of war? _____

Name _____

Find the Lucky Number

Directions: Find the average for each group of numbers.
Then, shade the triangle with the matching number.
The unshaded triangle contains the lucky number!

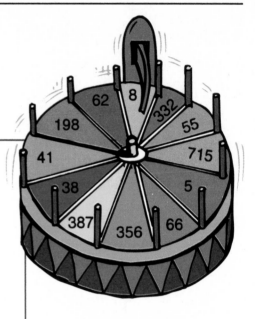

1. 64, 72, 99, 13 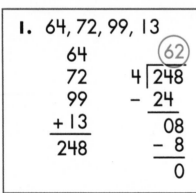	**2.** 5, 9, 7, 16, 3
3. 241, 123, 632	**4.** 22, 44, 66, 88	**5.** 522, 811, 812
6. 2, 5, 7, 4, 7	**7.** 68, 83, 47	**8.** 387, 451, 323
9. 17, 38, 59	**10.** 24, 40, 59	**11.** 293, 279, 111, 109

Divide It Up

Directions: Divide. Write the letter of each problem above its answer below.

I.	**I.**	**O.**	**D.**
34 $\overline{)2584}$	42 $\overline{)8526}$	63 $\overline{)6237}$	55 $\overline{)3575}$

D.	**Y.**	**T.**	**U.**
89 $\overline{)6319}$	90 $\overline{)1800}$	31 $\overline{)6231}$	18 $\overline{)882}$

___ ___ ___   ___ ___ ___   ___ ___ !
20   99   49   65   203   71   76   201

Directions: Find the total test scores below. Then, find the averages.

Students	Test Scores					Total	Average
Sue Ann	18	20	17	19	16		
James	15	14	17	16	13		
Tommy	19	19	20	18	19		
Carlos	16	19	18	17	16		
Anna	20	20	19	20	19		

Who has the highest average? _____

Who needs to study more? _____

Better Than the Average Team

The sports editor of your local newspaper needs your help averaging the team scores after the first five games of the season.

Directions: Solve to find the scoring average of each team.

Team	Points					Average
Bears	63	58	64	59	61	
Falcons	48	46	62	54	50	
Rams	49	54	46	57	49	
Eagles	70	71	67	62	65	
Red Hawks	65	68	60	61	61	
Cougars	62	56	57	68	52	
Wolverines	58	63	55	56	68	
Wildcats	52	56	54	49	54	

It All Averages Out!

Name _____

Directions: Solve the problems.

1. The Lumberjacks traveled 283 miles to Chicago for a game, 158 miles to Detroit, and 300 miles to New York. What was the average number of miles they traveled?

_____

2. The Hawks played 5 games. Use the chart below:

	1	2	3	4	5
Points scored	112	98	87	100	78

How many total points did they score? _____

What was the average points scored per game? _____

3. It took 40 minutes to play tennis match 1, 63 minutes to play match 2, and 68 minutes to play match 3.

How long did it take to play the entire game?

_____

What was the average length in minutes for each match?

_____

Keeping Track

Rob is training for the javelin throw at a big track meet. He wants to know how he is doing, so he records the distances of 10 throws he makes during practice.

Directions: Find Rob's average distance.

_____

Throw	Distance	Throw	Distance
1	23 feet	6	20 feet
2	26 feet	7	24 feet
3	21 feet	8	23 feet
4	23 feet	9	22 feet
5	25 feet	10	22 feet

The average of a group of numbers tells something about the main trend of the data. The three most important kinds of averages are called the **mode**, the **median**, and the **mean**.

The **mode** is the number in the data that occurs most often. The mode of the javelin distances is 23 feet, since that number appears three times—more often than any other does.

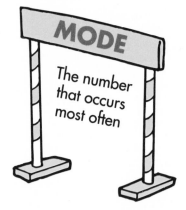

MODE

The number that occurs most often

If the data do not have a number that appears more than once, there is no mode. For example, the numbers 6, 4, 8, 7, 5, 3, and 9 have no mode.

A group of numbers can also have more than one mode. For example, the numbers 2, 5, 4, 3, 2, 3, and 6 have two modes since 2 and 3 both occur twice.

If a group of numbers does have a mode, the mode will always be one of the numbers in the list.

Keeping Track Again

Directions: Find the mode.

3, 6, 9, 5, 12, 5, 7, 8 _____

11, 7, 9, 11, 3, 8, 9, 10, 11 _____

8, 5, 6, 4, 7, 11, 10, 9 _____   5, 7, −2, 4, −5 , −2, 0, 2, 1 _____

4, 7, 5, 6, 7, 4, 3, 4, 8, 4, 7, 7 _____   3, 4, 3, 2, 0, 0, 1, 2, 0, 1 _____

3, 3, 3, 3, 3, 3, 3, 3, 3, 3 _____   1, 2, 3, 4, 5, 6, 7, 8, 9 _____

1, 2, 3, 1, 2, 3, 1, 2, 3, 1, 2, 3 _____   13, 12, 10, 15, 12, 14, 12, 11 _____

Directions: Solve the problems.

1. All of Jill's throws landed 24 feet away. What is the mode? _____

2. On page 21, look at Rob's data for his first ten throws.
How far would he have to throw the javelin on the
11th throw so that the data would have two modes? _____

3. Write a list of 6 numbers that have no mode. _____

4. Which javelin thrower below had a higher mode? _____

Kate	Adam
22 feet	21 feet
23	20
24	23
24	24
21	21
22	22
22	25

Jumping the Median

The **median** is another kind of average. When ordering a list of numbers from least to greatest, the median is the number that falls in the middle. Look at Anna's maximum high jumps for the last week.

Day	Height
Monday	62 inches
Tuesday	64 inches
Wednesday	62 inches
Thursday	64 inches
Friday	60 inches
Saturday	61 inches
Sunday	64 inches

Order the numbers: 60, 61, 62, **62**, 64, 64, 64. The number **62** falls in the middle. It is the median.

The mode is 64 inches. In some cases, the median and mode are the same number.

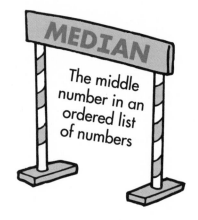

MEDIAN

The middle number in an ordered list of numbers

If there is an even number of heights, there will be two numbers in the middle. To find the median, add the two middle numbers and divide the sum by 2.

Example: 2, 2, 3, 4, 6, 6, 7, 9

The numbers **4** and **6** are both in the middle. $4 + 6 = 10$; $10 \div 2 = 5$. The median is **5**. The median does not have to be a number in the list.

Directions: Find the median.

3, 6, 9, 5, 12, 5, 8 _____

11, 7, 9, 11, 3, 8, 9, 10 _____

11, 6, 4, 7, 5, 9, 11, 10 _____

–4, 2, –3, –1, 1, –1, –2 _____

7, 5, 6, 4, 7, 11, 10, 9 _____

2, 4, 6, 8, 10, 12, 14, 16 _____

3, 3, 3, 3, 3, 3, 3, 3, 3, 3 _____

0, 1, 4, –2, 3, –1, –2 _____

55, 34, 67, 39, 47, 18, 46, 55, 61 _____

2, –2, 1, –1, 3, –4 _____

What Do You Mean?

Probably the most common average is the **mean**. To find the mean, add all the numbers in the list. Then, divide the sum by the total number of addends.

Suppose a hurdler completes his trials in the following times. Find the mean.

Trial	Time in Seconds
1	35
2	29
3	34
4	30
5	31
6	33

MEAN

The sum of all the numbers divided by the number of addends

Add the numbers: $35 + 29 + 34 + 30 + 31 + 33 = 192$
Divide 192 by 6 because there are 6 numbers in the list: $192 \div 6 = 32$.
The mean is 32 seconds.

The mean may or may not be a number in the list. The mean may also be different from the median and/or the mode.

Directions: Find the mean.

3, 6, 9, 5, 12 _____   11, 5, 9, 11, 3, 7, 9, 9 _____

3, 1, 0, 2, 0, 0 _____   4, 6, –1, –1 _____

–3, –2, –3, –1, –1 _____   2, –1, 1, –2 _____

3, 3, 3, 3, 3, 3, 3, 3, 3, 3 _____   5, 9, 6, 2, 7, 9, 12, 4, 8, 8 _____

9, 4, 5, 2, 6, 0, 3, 4, 3 _____   6, 7, 3, 6, 4, 2, 7, 5 _____

What Do You Mean by Median?

The **mean** is the average found by adding all values and dividing by the number of values. The **median** is the number that is exactly in the middle of the data.

Example: Lenny loves basketball. He scored the following points per game.

Game	Points
#1	5
#2	10
#3	3
#4	14
#5	3

Median: 3, 3, ⑤, 10, 14
  The median is 5 points per game.

Mean: 5 + 10 + 3 + 14 + 3 = 35
  35 ÷ 5 = 7
  The mean is an average of 7 points per game.

Directions: Study the data to correctly answer the questions.

Student	No. of Books Read
Anna	9
Carlos	5
Brian	7
Jada	8
Lin	11

1. List the numbers you would add and what you would divide them by to determine the mean number of books read by each student.

   _____

2. What is the mean? _____

3. What is the median? _____

Tanya's scout troop made beaded animals to sell and raise funds for a camping trip.

Troop Members	No. of Bead Animals Made
Tanya	17
Cho	15
María	11
Avishai	14
Lucy	9
Kely	6
Yong	21
Maya	6
Beth	9

4. List the numbers you would add and what you would divide them by to determine the mean number of beaded animals made by each troop member.

   _____

   _____

5. What is the mean? _____

6. What is the median? _____

Finding Mean

Directions: Read the passage and answer the questions.

What is the average number of people who walk by your house between 3:00 P.M. and 4:00 P.M. during the week? Are you interested in finding out the answer to this question? You'll need to find the **mean**, or average, of the numbers. If you record that 25 people pass by on Monday, 32 people pass by on Tuesday, 34 people pass by on Wednesday, 18 people pass by on Thursday, and 31 people pass by on Friday, you have gathered the information you need. To answer the question, you will need to find the average of all five numbers. Start by finding the sum of all five numbers. Then, divide the sum by 5 to find the average number of people who walk by your house each day between 3:00 P.M. and 4:00 P.M. Based on the information gathered above, the average number of people who walk by is 28.

1. Write a definition for the word **mean**.

_____

_____

2. What should you do after you find the sum of all five numbers?

_____

_____

3. What would you need to do first if you wanted to find the average number of people who walked by your house between 9:00 A.M. and 10:00 A.M.?

_____

_____

4. What does "28" answer in the article above?

_____

_____

5. Find the mean of the following five numbers: 65, 34, 76, 54, and 66.

_____

_____

Answer Key

Multiplication Fact Finder

Directions: Circle groups of numbers that make multiplication facts. Look horizontally and vertically.

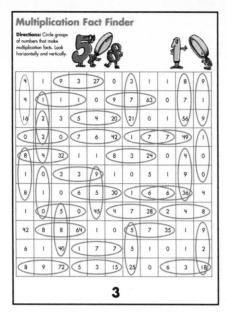

4	1	9	3	27	0	3	1	1	8	9
4	1	1	1	0	9	7	63	0	7	1
16	2	3	5	4	20	21	0	1	56	9
0	2	0	7	6	42	1	7	7	49	1
8	4	32	1	1	8	3	24	1	4	0
1	0	3	3	9	1	0	5	1	9	0
8	1	0	6	5	30	1	6	6	36	4
1	0	5	0	45	4	7	28	2	4	8
42	8	8	64	1	0	5	7	35	1	9
6	1	40	1	7	5	1	0	1	2	8
8	9	72	5	3	15	25	0	6	3	18

3

Cobwebs

Directions: Write each missing factor. The product is on the outside ring. Color sections of each web with even numbers yellow. Color sections of each web with odd numbers green.

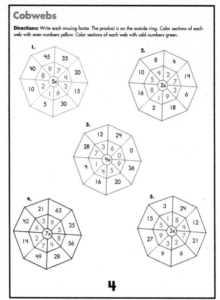

4

A New Team in Town

Did you know the Boston Bisons joined the Toledo Toucans to become a new NFL football team?

Directions: To find out what they are called now, solve each problem. Then, write the matching letter above the answer at the bottom of the page.

T	37 × 6 = 222	A	96 × 7 = 672	E	73 × 4 = 292	I	87 × 9 = 783	L	42 × 8 = 336

| S | 52 × 6 = 312 | F | 47 × 7 = 329 | H | 88 × 6 = 528 | L | 32 × 6 = 192 | U | 64 × 8 = 512 |

| L | 45 × 7 = 315 | F | 39 × 7 = 273 | B | 68 × 5 = 340 | O | 81 × 8 = 648 | B | 78 × 3 = 234 |

T H E   B U F F A L O
222 528 292   234 512 273 329 672 192 648

B I L L S
340 783 315 336 312

5

Number Letters

Each problem has a letter in place of a number.

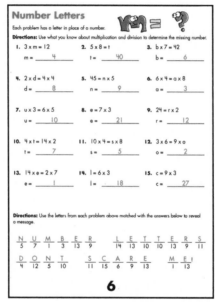

Directions: Use what you know about multiplication and division to determine the missing number.

1. 3 x m = 12   m = 4
2. 5 x 8 = t   t = 40
3. b x 7 = 42   b = 6
4. 2 x d = 4 x 4   d = 8
5. 45 = n x 5   n = 9
6. 6 x 4 = a x 8   a = 3
7. u x 3 = 6 x 5   u = 10
8. e = 7 x 3   e = 21
9. 24 = r x 2   r = 12
10. 4 x t = 14 x 2   t = 7
11. 10 x 4 = s x 8   s = 5
12. 3 x 6 = 9 x o   o = 2
13. 14 x e = 2 x 7   e = 1
14. l = 6 x 3   l = 18
15. c = 9 x 3   c = 27

Directions: Use the letters from each problem above matched with the answers below to reveal a message.

N U M B E R   L E T T E R S
5 7 1 3 13 9   14 13 10 10 13 9 11

D O N T   S C A R E   M E!
4 12 5 10   11 15 6 9 13   1 13

6

Add Them Up

> Multiplication is repeated addition.
> **Example:** 356 × 3 = 1,068   → 356 + 356 + 356 = 1,068

Directions: Rewrite each multiplication problem as an addition problem. Solve.

1. 576 × 4 = 2,304   → 576 + 576 + 576 + 576 = 2,304
2. 384 × 2 = 768   → 384 + 384 = 768
3. 907 × 3 = 2,721   → 907 + 907 + 907 = 2,721
4. 232 × 6 = 1,392   → 232 + 232 + 232 + 232 + 232 + 232 = 1,392
5. 843 × 4 = 3,372   → 843 + 843 + 843 + 843 = 3,372
6. 728 × 3 = 2,184   → 728 + 728 + 728 = 2,184
7. 912 × 5 = 4,560   → 912 + 912 + 912 + 912 + 912 = 4,560
8. 569 × 2 = 1,138   → 569 + 569 = 1,138
9. 206 × 7 = 1,442   → 206 + 206 + 206 + 206 + 206 + 206 + 206 = 1,442
10. 374 × 6 = 2,244   → 374 + 374 + 374 + 374 + 374 + 374 = 2,244

Think: With what type of problems would you find this strategy helpful?

7

Multiplication

Multiply 32 x 23.

	Step A	Step B		Step A	Step B
	32 × 2 = 64	32 × 20 = 640		32 × 23 = 96	32 × 23 = 96 (640)

since 2 x 32 = ___   then 20 x 32 = ___   3 x 32 = ___   20 x 32 = ___   **Step C** 640 + 96 = ___

Directions: Multiply.

	a.	b.	c.	d.	e.	f.	g.
1.	14 × 20 = 280	22 × 40 = 880	23 × 30 = 690	51 × 50 = 2,550	33 × 20 = 660	71 × 60 = 4,260	71 × 80 = 5,680
2.	32 × 40 = 1,280	21 × 30 = 630	41 × 70 = 2,870	51 × 70 = 3,570	31 × 90 = 2,790	31 × 60 = 1,860	61 × 50 = 3,050
3.	13 × 12 = 156	12 × 31 = 372	21 × 34 = 714	23 × 21 = 483	31 × 33 = 1,023	14 × 22 = 308	21 × 14 = 294
4.	23 × 23 = 529	21 × 44 = 924	42 × 12 = 504	21 × 13 = 273	11 × 41 = 451	22 × 24 = 528	33 × 32 = 1,056

8

Multiplying by a Two-Digit Number
With Regrouping

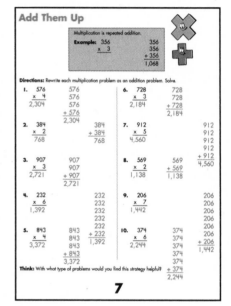

1. Multiply by the ones.
   8 x 7 = 56 (Carry the 5.)
2. Multiply by the ones.
   8 x 6 = 48 + 5 = 53
   (When they are completed, cross out all carried digits.)
   536
3. Multiply by the tens. Place a zero in the ones column.
   3 x 7 = 21 (Carry the 2.)
   536 10
4. Multiply by the tens.
   3 x 6 = 18 + 2 = 20
   536 2010
5. Add.
   536 + 2010 = 2,546
   67 × 38 = 2,546

Directions: Multiply.

37 × 24 = 888	77 × 21 = 1,617
23 × 45 = 1,035	54 × 38 = 2,052
48 × 62 = 2,976	67 × 29 = 1,943

Now, check your answers with a calculator.

9

Multiplication Practice

Directions: Multiply.

	a.	b.	c.	d.	e.
1.	89 ×21 = 1,869	58 ×92 = 5,336	97 ×53 = 5,141	63 ×80 = 5,040	76 ×10 = 760
2.	68 ×30 = 2,040	57 ×44 = 2,508	52 ×60 = 3,120	53 ×75 = 3,975	49 ×26 = 1,274
3.	74 ×50 = 3,700	74 ×89 = 6,586	62 ×97 = 6,014	69 ×40 = 2,760	54 ×38 = 2,052
4.	54 ×61 = 3,294	86 ×20 = 1,720	37 ×72 = 2,664	32 ×13 = 416	83 ×34 = 2,822
5.	43 ×66 = 2,838	85 ×88 = 7,480	65 ×55 = 3,575	54 ×78 = 4,212	38 ×47 = 1,786

10

Multiplication Drill

Directions: Multiply. Color the picture below by matching each number with its paintbrush.

134 ×22 = 2,948	48 ×66 = 3,168	876 ×13 = 11,388	432 ×64 = 27,648

68 ×11 = 748	5,478 ×8 = 43,824	248 ×61 = 15,128	6,897 ×6 = 41,382

82 ×4 = 328	6,798 ×5 = 33,990	79 ×86 = 6,794	694 ×38 = 26,372

11

Up, Up, and Away

Directions: Multiply. Put the letters of the answers on the lines below to find out a secret message.

J 159 × 47 = 7,473
T 454 × 60 = 27,240
G 719 × 18 = 12,942
I 106 × 85 = 9,010
O 295 × 65 = 19,175
R 607 × 45 = 27,315
E 599 × 12 = 7,188
B 333 × 65 = 21,645
A 682 × 23 = 15,686

G R E A T   J O B !
12,942 27,315 7,188 15,686 27,240   7,473 19,175 21,645 9,010

12

Multiplication With Three Numbers

Multiply 538 x 426.

Step A	Step B	Step C	Step D
538 ×426 / 3228	538 ×426 / 3228 10760	538 ×426 / 3228 10760 215200	538 ×426 / 3228 10760 215200 229,188
6 × 538 = 3,228	20 × 538 = 10,760	400 × 538 = 215,200	___ + ___ + ___ = 229,188

Directions: Multiply.

	a.	b.	c.	d.	e.
1.	294 ×473 = 139,062	397 ×245 = 97,265	215 ×169 = 36,335	852 ×386 = 328,872	415 ×352 = 146,080
2.	862 ×792 = 682,704	254 ×577 = 146,558	693 ×968 = 670,824	782 ×848 = 663,136	763 ×635 = 484,505

13

What Exactly Is Division?

In division, you begin with an amount of something (the dividend), separate it into small groups (the divisor), then find out how many groups are created (the quotient).

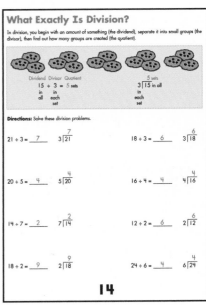

Dividend Divisor Quotient
15 ÷ 3 = 5 sets
in all   in each set

5 sets
3)15 in all

Directions: Solve these division problems.

21 ÷ 3 = 7   3)21 = 7
18 ÷ 3 = 6   3)18 = 6
20 ÷ 5 = 4   5)20 = 4
16 ÷ 4 = 4   4)16 = 4
14 ÷ 7 = 2   7)14 = 2
12 ÷ 2 = 6   2)12 = 6
18 ÷ 2 = 9   2)18 = 9
24 ÷ 6 = 4   6)24 = 4

14

A Rule to Live By

T 9)9 = 1	A 6)30 = 5	T 2)2 = 1
F 9)81 = 9	R 8)56 = 7	E 9)18 = 2	H 7)42 = 6
A 7)35 = 5	F 3)27 = 9	R 9)63 = 7	C 9)36 = 4
E 8)16 = 2	K 6)48 = 8	E 7)14 = 2	O 8)24 = 3
H 6)36 = 6	A 9)45 = 5	K 5)40 = 8	O 3)9 = 3
F 6)54 = 9	R 7)49 = 7	A 8)40 = 5	H 8)48 = 6

Directions: Write the letters on the lines to find a good rule to follow.

T A K E   C A R E   O F
1 5 8 2   4 5 7 2   3 9

T H E   E A R T H
1 6 2   2 5 7 1 6

15

Division

Divide 4)23.

Step A	Step B	Step C
5 ← 4)23 20 (5×4)	4)23 20 / 3 (23-20)	5 R3 4)23 20 / 3 (remainder)

Directions: Divide.

	a.	b.	c.	d.	e.	f.	g.
1.	7 R2 6)44 42 / 2	4 R2 9)38	3 R1 3)10	7 R1 2)15	1 R7 8)15	5 R2 9)47	3 R2 7)23
2.	3 R1 4)13	2 R1 7)15	2 R1 6)13	4 R4 5)24	3 R2 6)20	2 R4 8)20	2 R4 5)14
3.	4 R7 8)39	9 R1 2)19	3 R3 9)30	4 R4 7)32	3 R2 3)14	4 R2 8)34	2 R1 4)9
4.	5 R1 6)31	1 R3 9)12	4 R2 6)26	8 R1 2)17	2 R1 9)19	6 R1 5)31	5 R1 2)11
5.	5 R6 8)46	5 R6 7)41	5 R1 4)21	5 R1 3)16	6 R1 4)25	4 R2 5)22	6 R1 3)19

16

Division Drill

Divide 7) 949.

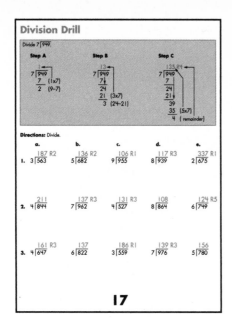

Step A
```
     7 ) 949
     7     (1×7)
     ‾
     2     (9-7)
```

Step B
```
       13
     7 ) 949
     7
     ‾
     24
     21    (3×7)
     ‾
      3    (24-21)
```

Step C
```
       135 R4
     7 ) 949
     7
     ‾
     24
     21
     ‾
     39
     35    (5×7)
     ‾
      4   ( remainder)
```

Directions: Divide.

	a.	b.	c.	d.	e.
1.	187 R2 3) 563	136 R2 5) 682	106 R1 9) 955	117 R3 8) 939	337 R1 2) 675
2.	211 4) 844	137 R3 7) 962	131 R3 4) 527	108 8) 864	124 R5 6) 749
3.	161 R3 4) 647	137 6) 822	186 R1 3) 559	139 R3 7) 976	156 5) 780

17

Table Tool

Directions: Fill in the multiplication table to the right.

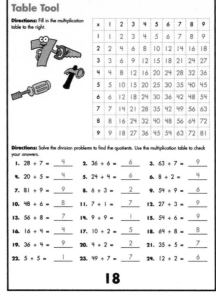

x	1	2	3	4	5	6	7	8	9
1	1	2	3	4	5	6	7	8	9
2	2	4	6	8	10	12	14	16	18
3	3	6	9	12	15	18	21	24	27
4	4	8	12	16	20	24	28	32	36
5	5	10	15	20	25	30	35	40	45
6	6	12	18	24	30	36	42	48	54
7	7	14	21	28	35	42	49	56	63
8	8	16	24	32	40	48	56	64	72
9	9	18	27	36	45	54	63	72	81

Directions: Solve the division problems to find the quotients. Use the multiplication table to check your answers.

1. 28 ÷ 7 = 4   2. 36 ÷ 6 = 6   3. 63 ÷ 7 = 9
4. 20 ÷ 5 = 4   5. 24 ÷ 4 = 6   6. 8 ÷ 2 = 4
7. 81 ÷ 9 = 9   8. 6 ÷ 3 = 2   9. 54 ÷ 9 = 6
10. 48 ÷ 6 = 8   11. 7 ÷ 1 = 7   12. 27 ÷ 3 = 9
13. 56 ÷ 8 = 7   14. 9 ÷ 9 = 1   15. 54 ÷ 6 = 9
16. 16 ÷ 4 = 4   17. 10 ÷ 2 = 5   18. 64 ÷ 8 = 8
19. 36 ÷ 4 = 9   20. 4 ÷ 2 = 2   21. 35 ÷ 5 = 7
22. 5 ÷ 5 = 1   23. 49 ÷ 7 = 7   24. 12 ÷ 2 = 6

18

Jersey Division

Directions: Write the numbers in the correct footballs to get the given answer.

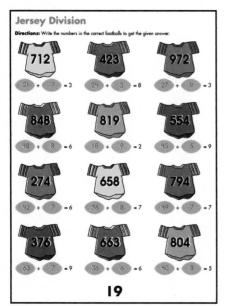

712	423	972
21 ÷ 7 = 3	24 ÷ 3 = 8	27 ÷ 9 = 3
848	**819**	**554**
48 ÷ 8 = 6	18 ÷ 9 = 2	45 ÷ 5 = 9
274	**658**	**794**
42 ÷ 7 = 6	56 ÷ 8 = 7	49 ÷ 7 = 7
376	**663**	**804**
63 ÷ 7 = 9	36 ÷ 6 = 6	40 ÷ 8 = 5

19

Round and Round

Directions: Divide. Then, use the code to solve the riddle.

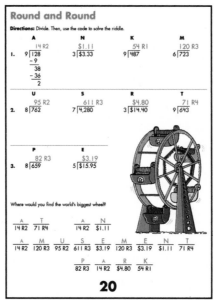

	A	N	K	M
1.	14 R2 9) 128 - 9 ‾ 38 - 36 ‾ 2	$1.11 3) $3.33	54 R1 9) 487	120 R3 6) 723

	U	S	R	T
2.	95 R2 8) 762	611 R3 7) 4,280	$4.80 3) $14.40	71 R4 9) 643

	P	E
3.	82 R3 8) 659	$3.19 5) $15.95

Where would you find the world's biggest wheel?

```
 A    T       A    N
14 R2 71 R4  14 R2 $1.11

 A      M      U      S      E      M      E      N      T
14 R2 120 R3 95 R2 611 R3 $3.19 120 R3 $3.19 $1.11 71 R4

 P     A    R     K
82 R3 14 R2 $4.80 54 R1
```

20

Doggie Trouble

Directions: Help the dog get to its bone by connecting the correctly done division problems to make a path.

85 R17 23) 1972	30 R29 32) 989	14 R27 43) 629	232 R3 30) 6963	107 R4 65) 6959
104 R8 15) 1508	31 R4 22) 687	31 R12 19) 582	78 R6 87) 6933	155 R11 52) 8071
255 R15 31) 8013	14 R15 42) 6231	20 R18 26) 541	54 R9 18) 819	31 R3 26) 809
52 R27 60) 3207	158 R31 39) 6193	36 R11 27) 983	115 R8 71) 8203	58 R3 17) 989
	18 R26 81) 1484	44 R7 44) 1943	63 R9 28) 1773	

21

Wh-o-o-o Knows?

Directions: Find the quotients and the remainders.

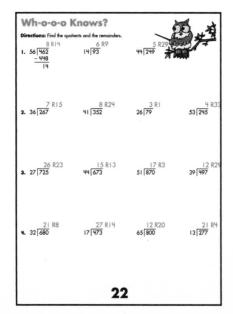

1.	8 R14 56) 462 - 448 ‾ 14	6 R9 14) 93	5 R29 44) 249
2.	7 R15 36) 267	8 R24 41) 352	3 R1 26) 79	4 R33 53) 245
3.	26 R23 27) 725	15 R13 44) 673	17 R3 51) 870	12 R29 39) 497
4.	21 R8 32) 680	27 R14 17) 473	12 R20 65) 800	21 R4 13) 277

22

Hmmm, What Should I Do?

Example: 52 (+) 9 = 61

8 (×) 4 = 32

Directions: Write the correct symbols in the circles.

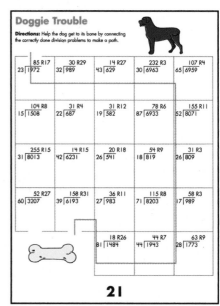

7 (×) 8 = 56   81 (−) 6 = 75   55 (−) 3 = 52

54 (÷) 9 = 6   2 (×) 1 = 2   40 (−) 2 = 38

36 (−) 5 = 31   0 (+) 2 = 2   8 (×) 8 = 64

12 (+) 6 = 18   9 (×) 8 = 72   18 (+) 5 = 23

72 (−) 7 = 65   32 (+) 5 = 37

0 (×) 1 = 0   48 (÷) 6 = 8

9 (×) 1 = 9   32 (÷) 4 = 8

45 (÷) 9 = 5   6 (×) 7 = 42

23

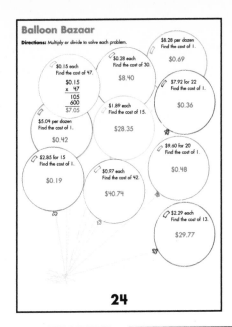

Balloon Bazaar

Directions: Multiply or divide to solve each problem.

$0.15 each
Find the cost of 47.

$0.15
× 47
105
600
$7.05

$0.28 each
Find the cost of 30.

$8.40

$8.28 per dozen
Find the cost of 1.

$0.69

$7.92 for 22
Find the cost of 1.

$0.36

$1.89 each
Find the cost of 15.

$28.35

$5.04 per dozen
Find the cost of 1.

$0.42

$9.60 for 20
Find the cost of 1.

$0.48

$2.85 for 15
Find the cost of 1.

$0.19

$0.97 each
Find the cost of 42.

$40.74

$2.29 each
Find the cost of 13.

$29.77

24

Number Puzzles

Directions: Solve these number puzzles.   Sample answers are given.

1	
Write your age.	9
Multiply it by 3.	27
Add 18.	45
Multiply by 2.	90
Subtract 36.	54
Divide by 6. (your age)	9

2	
Write any number.	31
Double that number.	62
Add 15.	77
Double again.	154
Subtract 30.	124
Divide by 2.	62
Divide by 2 again.	31

3	
Write any 2-digit number.	46
Double that number.	92
Add 43.	135
Subtract 18.	117
Add 11.	128
Divide by 2.	64
Subtract 18.	46

4	
Write the number of children in your neighborhood.	5
Double that number.	10
Add 15.	25
Double it again.	50
Subtract 30.	20
Divide by 4.	5

25

Mary Anning

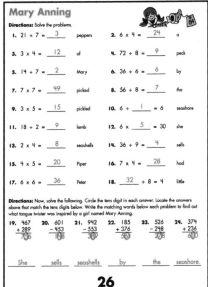

Directions: Solve the problems.

1. 21 ÷ 7 = __3__ peppers
2. 6 × 4 = __24__ a
3. 3 × 4 = __12__ of
4. 72 ÷ 8 = __9__ peck
5. 14 ÷ 7 = __2__ Mary
6. 36 ÷ 6 = __6__ by
7. 7 × 7 = __49__ picked
8. 56 ÷ 8 = __7__ the
9. 3 × 5 = __15__ pickled
10. 6 ÷ __1__ = 6 seashore
11. 18 ÷ 2 = __9__ lamb
12. 6 × __5__ = 30 she
13. 2 × 4 = __8__ seashells
14. 36 ÷ 9 = __4__ sells
15. 4 × 5 = __20__ Piper
16. 7 × 4 = __28__ had
17. 6 × 6 = __36__ Peter
18. __32__ ÷ 8 = 4 little

Directions: Now, solve the following. Circle the tens digit in each answer. Locate the answers above that match the tens digits below. Write the matching words below each problem to find out what tongue twister was inspired by a girl named Mary Anning.

19. 467 + 289 756	20. 601 – 453 148	21. 942 – 553 389	22. 185 + 376 561	23. 526 – 248 278	24. 374 + 236 610
She	sells	seashells	by	the	seashore.

26

Comparisons

Directions: Circle the symbol that makes the statement true.

1. 14 + 22 ⓥ > ⓥ 20 + 11
2. 48 ÷ 4 ⓥ < ⓥ = 6 + 7
3. (5 × 5) + 25 < > ⓥ= 100 – 50
4. 77 + 20 – 6 ⓥ > ⓥ = 33 + 33 + 33

Directions: Use at least two numbers and an operation to complete the statements below.

5. 9 × 8 < __Answers will vary.__
6. 72 – 34 > __Answers will vary.__
7. 18 ÷ 96 > __Answers will vary.__
8. 231 + 57 < __Answers will vary.__

Directions: Replace each shape with a number to make the statements true.

9. ■ – 8 < 10
10. 26 + ▲ = 73

■ = __any < 18__   ▲ = __47__

11. 12 ÷ 6 > ▱
12. ● × 3 < 9

▱ = __any < 2__   ● = __any < 3__

Explaining

Look at problems 9–12. Which problems will have more than one solution? Why?

All but problem 10 has more than 1 solution because of the < and > signs.

27

Add and Subtract Story Problems

Directions: Find the answers. Show your work.

1. Jenny bought 146 gum balls.
   She gave some to her sister.
   She had 102 gum balls left.
   How many gum balls did she give to her sister?

   146
   – 102
   44   44

2. Allen counted 45 boys and 33 girls on the school bus.
   How many children were on the bus?

   45
   + 33
   78   78

   How many more boys were on the bus?

   45
   – 33
   12   12

3. Marta counted 988 jelly beans.
   Sixty-one jelly beans were yellow.
   How many were not yellow?

   988
   – 61
   927   927

4. Juan's school meeting room can hold 382 people.
   There are 252 people in the room.
   How many more people can it hold?

   382
   – 252
   130   130

5. Amy and Kathy went bowling.
   Amy had 212 points. Kathy had 255 points.
   How many points did they have altogether?

   212
   + 255
   467   467

   How many more points did Kathy have?

   255
   – 212
   43   43

6. There were 509 people at the basketball game.
   One hundred of those people were children.
   How many of the people were not children?

   509
   – 100
   409   409

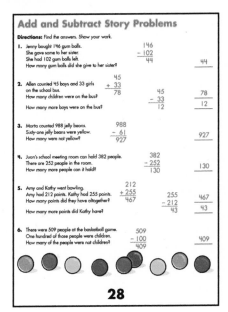

28

Wordy Problems

Directions: Solve each problem.

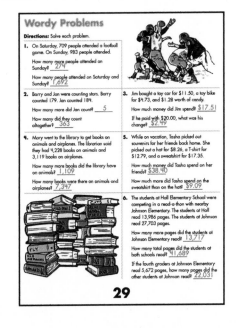

1. On Saturday, 709 people attended a football game. On Sunday, 983 people attended.
   How many more people attended on Sunday? __274__
   How many people attended on Saturday and Sunday? __1,692__

2. Barry and Jan were counting stars. Barry counted 179. Jan counted 184.
   How many more did Jan count? __5__
   How many did they count altogether? __363__

3. Jim bought a toy car for $11.50, a toy bike for $4.73, and $1.28 worth of candy.
   How much money did Jim spend? __$17.51__
   If he paid with $20.00, what was his change? __$2.49__

4. Mary went to the library to get books on animals and airplanes. The librarian said they had 4,228 books on animals and 3,119 books on airplanes.
   How many more books did the library have on animals? __1,109__
   How many books were there on animals and airplanes? __7,347__

5. While on vacation, Tasha picked out souvenirs for her friends back home. She picked out a hat for $8.26, a T-shirt for $12.79, and a sweatshirt for $17.35.
   How much money did Tasha spend on her friends? __$38.40__
   How much more did Tasha spend on the sweatshirt than on the hat? __$9.09__

6. The students at Hall Elementary School were competing in a read-a-thon with nearby Johnson Elementary. The students at Hall read 13,986 pages. The students at Johnson read 27,703 pages.
   How many more pages did the students at Johnson Elementary read? __13,717__
   How many total pages did the students at both schools read? __41,689__
   If the fourth graders at Johnson Elementary read 5,672 pages, how many pages did the other students at Johnson read? __22,031__

29

Par for the Course

Directions: Solve these problems by writing an equation. Remember to label your answer. (You may use a calculator and the information below to help.)

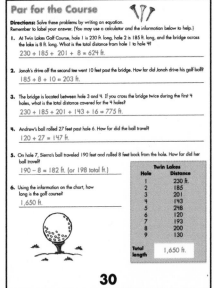

1. At Twin Lakes Golf Course, hole 1 is 230 ft. long, hole 2 is 185 ft. long, and the bridge across the lake is 8 ft. long. What is the total distance from hole 1 to hole 4?
   230 + 185 + 201 + 8 = 624 ft.

2. Jonah's drive off the second tee went 10 feet past the bridge. How far did Jonah drive his golf ball?
   185 + 8 + 10 = 203 ft.

3. The bridge is located between hole 3 and 4. If you cross the bridge twice during the first 4 holes, what is the total distance covered for the 4 holes?
   230 + 185 + 201 + 143 + 16 = 775 ft.

4. Andrew's ball rolled 27 feet past hole 6. How far did the ball travel?
   120 + 27 = 147 ft.

5. On hole 7, Sierra's ball traveled 190 feet and rolled 8 feet back from the hole. How far did her ball travel?
   190 – 8 = 182 ft. (or 198 total ft.)

6. Using the information on the chart, how long is the golf course?
   1,650 ft.

Twin Lakes	
Hole	Distance
1	230 ft.
2	185
3	201
4	143
5	120
6	193
7	200
8	130
Total length	1,650 ft.

30

Wacky Waldo's Snow Show

Wacky Waldo's Snow Show is an exciting and fantastic sight. Waldo has trained whales and bears to skate together on the ice. There is a hockey game between a team of sharks and a team of wolves. Elephants ride sleds down steep hills. Horses and buffaloes ski swiftly down mountains.

Directions: Write each problem and its answer.

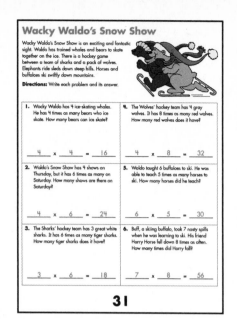

1. Wacky Waldo has 4 ice-skating whales. He has 4 times as many bears who ice skate. How many bears can ice skate?

___4___ x ___4___ = ___16___

2. Waldo's Snow Show has 4 shows on Thursday, but it has 6 times as many on Saturday. How many shows are there on Saturday?

___4___ x ___6___ = ___24___

3. The Sharks' hockey team has 3 great white sharks. It has 6 times as many tiger sharks. How many tiger sharks does it have?

___3___ x ___6___ = ___18___

4. The Wolves' hockey team has 4 gray wolves. It has 8 times as many red wolves. How many red wolves does it have?

___4___ x ___8___ = ___32___

5. Waldo taught 6 buffaloes to ski. He was able to teach 5 times as many horses to ski. How many horses did he teach?

___6___ x ___5___ = ___30___

6. Buff, a skiing buffalo, took 7 nasty spills when he was learning to ski. His friend Harry Horse fell down 8 times as often. How many times did Harry fall?

___7___ x ___8___ = ___56___

31

Multiplying With Molly

Directions: Write the problem and the answer for each question.

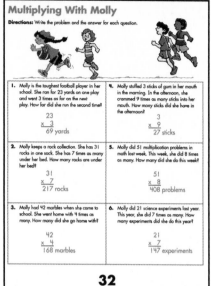

1. Molly is the toughest football player in her school. She ran for 23 yards on one play and went 3 times as far on the next play. How far did she run the second time?

23
x 3
69 yards

2. Molly keeps a rock collection. She has 31 rocks in one sack. She has 7 times as many under her bed. How many rocks are under her bed?

31
x 7
217 rocks

3. Molly had 42 marbles when she came to school. She went home with 4 times as many. How many did she go home with?

42
x 4
168 marbles

4. Molly stuffed 3 sticks of gum in her mouth in the morning. In the afternoon, she crammed 9 times as many sticks into her mouth. How many sticks did she have in the afternoon?

3
x 9
27 sticks

5. Molly did 51 multiplication problems in math last week. This week, she did 8 times as many. How many did she do this week?

51
x 8
408 problems

6. Molly did 21 science experiments last year. This year, she did 7 times as many. How many experiments did she do this year?

21
x 7
147 experiments

32

Step by Step

Directions: Read the problems below. Write each answer in the space provided.

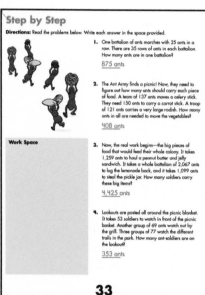

1. One battalion of ants marches with 25 ants in a row. There are 35 rows of ants in each battalion. How many ants are in one battalion?

875 ants

2. The Ant Army finds a picnic! Now, they need to figure out how many ants should carry each piece of food. A team of 137 ants moves a celery stick. They need 150 ants to carry a carrot stick. A troop of 121 ants carries a very large radish. How many ants in all are needed to move the vegetables?

408 ants

Work Space

3. Now, the real work begins—the big pieces of food that would feed their whole colony. It takes 1,259 ants to haul a peanut butter and jelly sandwich. It takes a whole battalion of 2,067 ants to lug the lemonade back, and it takes 1,099 ants to steal the pickle jar. How many soldiers carry these big items?

4,425 ants

4. Lookouts are posted all around the picnic blanket. It takes 53 soldiers to watch in front of the picnic basket. Another group of 69 ants watch out by the grill. Three groups of 77 watch the different trails in the park. How many ant-soldiers are on the lookout?

353 ants

33

Bargain Bonanza at Pat's Pet Place

Directions: Pat is having a gigantic sale. Help him divide his animals into groups for the sale.

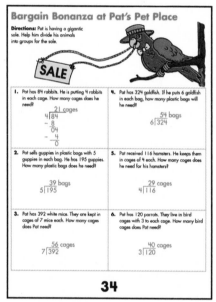

SALE

1. Pat has 84 rabbits. He is putting 4 rabbits in each cage. How many cages does he need?

21 cages
4⟌84
−8
04
−4
0

2. Pat sells guppies in plastic bags with 5 guppies in each bag. He has 195 guppies. How many plastic bags does he need?

39 bags
5⟌195

3. Pat has 392 white mice. They are kept in cages of 7 mice each. How many cages does Pat need?

56 cages
7⟌392

4. Pat has 324 goldfish. If he puts 6 goldfish in each bag, how many plastic bags will he need?

54 bags
6⟌324

5. Pat received 116 hamsters. He keeps them in cages of 4 each. How many cages does he need for his hamsters?

29 cages
4⟌116

6. Pat has 120 parrots. They live in bird cages with 3 to each cage. How many bird cages does Pat need?

40 cages
3⟌120

34

Humpback Whales

Directions: Solve the following word problems.

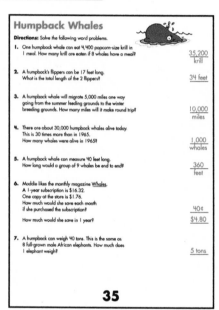

1. One humpback whale can eat 4,400 popcorn-size krill in 1 meal. How many krill are eaten if 8 whales have a meal?

35,200 krill

2. A humpback's flippers can be 17 feet long. What is the total length of the 2 flippers?

34 feet

3. A humpback whale will migrate 5,000 miles one way going from the summer feeding grounds to the winter breeding grounds. How many miles will it make round trip?

10,000 miles

4. There are about 30,000 humpback whales alive today. This is 30 times more than in 1965. How many whales were alive in 1965?

1,000 whales

5. A humpback whale can measure 40 feet long. How long would a group of 9 whales be end to end?

360 feet

6. Maddie likes the monthly magazine Whales. A 1-year subscription is $16.32. One copy at the store is $1.76. How much would she save each month if she purchased the subscription?

40¢

How much would she save in 1 year?

$4.80

7. A humpback can weigh 40 tons. This is the same as 8 full-grown male African elephants. How much does 1 elephant weigh?

5 tons

35

Story Problems

Directions: Read the problems and solve by multiplying or dividing.

1. Mrs. Webb drives a total of 25 miles to and from work each day. She works 5 days a week. How many miles does she drive each week?

125 mi.

2. The Produce Company sent Jack's Market 3 boxes of apples. Each box weighed 83 pounds. How much did the 3 boxes weigh?

249 lb.

3. Mrs. Barry baked 24 cookies for her 4 children. How many cookies did each child receive?

6

4. David delivers 901 newspapers each week. How many newspapers will he deliver in 9 weeks?

8,109

5. Henry read 56 pages each day for three days. How many pages did he read in 3 days?

168

6. Karen and Barbara have 138 books to organize. How many books will they each have if they divide the books equally?

69

7. The post office has 864 letters to deliver. There are 8 mail carriers. How many letters will each mail carrier deliver?

108

8. Tommy practices piano for 55 minutes each day. How many minutes does she practice in 65 days?

3,575

9. Mr. Adams makes $8.25 each hour. How much does he make in 8 hours?

$66

36

Which Problem Is Correct?

Directions: Circle the equation on the left you should use to solve the problem. Then, solve the problem. Remember the decimal point in money questions. Add the dollar signs ($) to those answers.

1.
56
+ 17

56
− 17
39

Bill and his friends collect baseball cards. Bill has 17 fewer cards than Mack. Bill has 56 cards. How many baseball cards does Mack have?

39 cards

2.
54
x 3
162

3⟌54

Amos bought 54 baseball cards. He already has 3 times as many. How many baseball cards did Amos have before his latest purchase?

162 cards

3.
3.80
+3.50

3.80
−3.50
30

Joe paid $3.50 for a Mickey Mantle baseball card. Ted Williams cost him $3.80. How much more did he pay for Ted Williams than for Mickey Mantle?

$0.30 more

4.
3.60
x 9

40
9⟌3.60

Will bought 9 baseball cards for $3.60. How much did he pay per (for each) card?

$0.40 per card

5.
8.00
+ .50

8.00
− .50
7.50

Babe Ruth baseball cards were selling for $8.00. Herb Score baseball cards sold for 50 cents. Herb Score cards sold for how much less than Babe Ruth cards?

$7.50 less

6.
0.75
x 8
6.00

8⟌0.75

Andy bought 8 baseball cards at 75 cents each. How much did Andy pay in all?

$6.00 in all

37

Map Story Problems

Directions: Use this map of California to help you answer questions. Show your work on another sheet of paper.

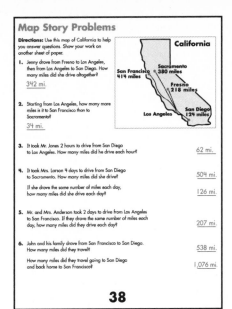

California

San Francisco 414 miles
Sacramento 380 miles
Fresno 218 miles
Los Angeles
San Diego 124 miles

1. Jenny drove from Fresno to Los Angeles, then from Los Angeles to San Diego. How many miles did she drive altogether?
   342 mi.

2. Starting from Los Angeles, how many more miles is it to San Francisco than to Sacramento?
   34 mi.

3. It took Mr. Jones 2 hours to drive from San Diego to Los Angeles. How many miles did he drive each hour?
   62 mi.

4. It took Mrs. Larson 4 days to drive from San Diego to Sacramento. How many miles did she drive?
   504 mi.

   If she drove the same number of miles each day, how many miles did she drive each day?
   126 mi.

5. Mr. and Mrs. Anderson took 2 days to drive from Los Angeles to San Francisco. If they drove the same number of miles each day, how many miles did they drive each day?
   207 mi.

6. John and his family drove from San Francisco to San Diego. How many miles did they travel?
   538 mi.

   How many miles did they travel going to San Diego and back home to San Francisco?
   1,076 mi.

38

Perplexing Problems

Directions: Solve these problems.

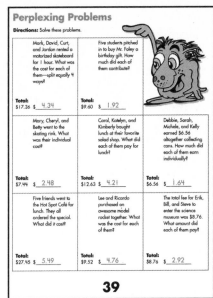

Mark, David, Curt, and Jordan rented a motorized skateboard for 1 hour. What was the cost for each of them—split equally 4 ways?	Five students pitched in to buy Mr. Foley a birthday gift. How much did each of them contribute?
Total: $17.36 $ 4.34	**Total:** $9.60 $ 1.92

Mary, Cheryl, and Betty went to the skating rink. What was their individual cost?	Carol, Katelyn, and Kimberly bought lunch at their favorite salad shop. What did each of them pay for lunch?	Debbie, Sarah, Michele, and Kelly earned $6.56 altogether collecting cans. How much did each of them earn individually?
Total: $7.44 $ 2.48	**Total:** $12.63 $ 4.21	**Total:** $6.56 $ 1.64

Five friends went to the Hot Spot Café for lunch. They all ordered the special. What did it cost?	Lee and Ricardo purchased an awesome model rocket together. What was the cost for each of them?	The total fee for Erik, Bill, and Steve to enter the science museum was $8.76. What amount did each of them pay?
Total: $27.45 $ 5.49	**Total:** $9.52 $ 4.76	**Total:** $8.76 $ 2.92

39

A Day at the Ballpark

CONCESSION FOOD
Peanuts	$1.50
Popcorn	$1.25
Cola small	$1.00
medium	$1.75
large	$2.25
Caramel corn	$2.00
Hot dog	$1.75
Candy bar	$1.00
Pizza	$2.50

TICKETS
	Adults	Children (12)
Box seats	$28.00	$12.00
Reserved	$18.00	$9.00
Bleachers	$8.00	$4.00

Directions: Solve the problems.

1. The Miller family, Mr. Miller, Mrs. Miller, 9-year-old Sarah, and 13-year-old David, went to the ballpark to cheer for their favorite team.

   How much would it cost if they sat in the box seats? $96.00
   How much if they sat in the reserved seats? $63.00
   How much if they sat in the bleachers? $28.00

2. Dad wants to buy a hot dog, large cola, and a bag of peanuts. How much will it cost if there is no tax? $5.50

3. Dad bought a pizza and a small cola for each person in the family. How much did he spend? $14.00

4. Make up a "Day at the Ballpark" story problem of your own. Exchange it with a friend.
   _____
   Answers will vary.

40

Too Much Information

Directions: Sometimes there is too much information. Cross out the information not needed and solve the problems.

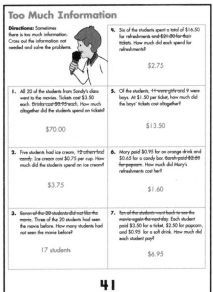

4. Six of the students spent a total of $16.50 for refreshments and $21.00 for their tickets. How much did each spend on refreshments?
   $2.75

1. All 20 of the students from Sandy's class went to the movies. Tickets cost $3.50 each. Drinks cost $0.95 each. How much altogether did the students spend on tickets?
   $70.00

5. Of the students, 11 were girls and 9 were boys. At $1.50 per ticket, how much did the boys' tickets cost altogether?
   $13.50

2. Five students had ice cream, 12 others had candy. Ice cream cost $0.75 per cup. How much did the students spend on ice cream?
   $3.75

6. Mary paid $0.95 for an orange drink and $0.65 for a candy bar. Sarah paid $2.50 for popcorn. How much did Mary's refreshments cost her?
   $1.60

3. Seven of the 20 students did not like the movie. Three of the 20 students had seen the movie before. How many students had not seen the movie before?
   17 students

7. Ten of the students went back to see the movie again the next day. Each student paid $3.50 for a ticket, $2.50 for popcorn, and $0.95 for a soft drink. How much did each student pay?
   $6.95

41

Money Matters

Directions: Find the answers.

1. Janet went to the store and bought meat for $2.20 and bread for eighty cents. How much did she spend at the store? $3.00

2. Amy had $4.30. She spent $1.99 on a game. How much did she have left? $2.31

3. Brad earned $5.00 mowing lawns. He spent $1.10 and saved the rest. How much did Brad save? $3.90

4. Cora earns $4.50 a week for babysitting. How much will she make in 4 weeks? $18.00

5. Twenty people each spent $5.98 for dinner. How much money did they spend altogether? $119.60

6. Mrs. Smith gave Jay $3.10 to spend at the fair. He returned with eleven cents. How much money did Jay spend at the fair? $2.99

7. Sammy saved $7.58 in March and $8.56 in April. How did Sammy save in the two months? $16.14
   How much more did he save in April? $.98

8. Martha makes $1.19 each day. How much did Martha make in 28 days? $33.32

9. Larry has $3.66. His older brother Scott has $6.56. How much do they have together? $10.22
   How much more does Scott have? $2.90

10. Roger earns $2.50 helping his dad at the store each day. How much will Roger have after 45 days? $112.50

42

A 5-Step Formula

5-Step Formula	Step 1: What is the question?
	Step 2: What facts are important?
	Step 3: What information is not needed?
	Step 4: What operation (+, –, x, or ÷) should be used?
	Step 5: Use the operation and the important information to solve the problem.

Directions: Use the 5-step formula.

A squirrel can run 12 mph over a short distance. An elephant can run 25 mph. An ostrich can run 15 mph faster than an elephant. How fast can an ostrich run?

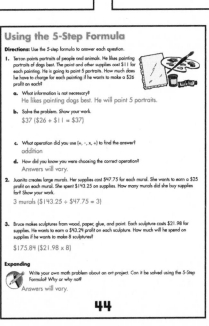

1. What question are you being asked to answer?
   How fast can an ostrich run?

2. Underline the important information. Write that information here.
   An elephant runs 25 mph. An ostrich runs 15 mph faster than an elephant.

3. Cross out the information that is not needed.
   A squirrel can run 12 mph.

4. What words in the problem help you decide which operation to use?
   "faster than"

5. Solve the problem. Show your work.
   40 mph (25 + 15 = 40)

Reflecting

You might need to read a problem more than once to complete the 5-step formula. What will be different about each time you read the problem?

Each time you read the problem you are looking for the answer to a different question from the 5-step formula.

43

Using the 5-Step Formula

Directions: Use the 5-step formula to answer each question.

1. Terron paints portraits of people and animals. He likes painting portraits of dogs best. The paint and other supplies cost $11 for each painting. He is going to paint 5 portraits. How much does he have to charge for each painting if he wants to make a $26 profit on each?

   a. What information is not necessary?
      He likes painting dogs best. He will paint 5 portraits.

   b. Solve the problem. Show your work.
      $37 ($26 + $11 = $37)

   c. What operation did you use (+, –, x, ÷) to find the answer?
      addition

   d. How did you know you were choosing the correct operation?
      Answers will vary.

2. Juanita creates large murals. Her supplies cost $47.75 for each mural. She wants to earn a $25 profit on each mural. She spent $143.25 on supplies. How many murals did she buy supplies for? Show your work.
   3 murals ($143.25 ÷ $47.75 = 3)

3. Bruce makes sculptures from wood, paper, glue, and paint. Each sculpture costs $21.98 for supplies. He wants to earn a $43.24 profit on each sculpture. How much will he spend on supplies if he wants to make 8 sculptures?
   $175.84 ($21.98 x 8)

Expanding

Write your own math problem about an art project. Can it be solved using the 5-Step Formula? Why or why not?
Answers will vary.

44

Leftovers

Sometimes you must think about the meaning of the **remainder** of a division problem. If the answer must be a whole number, then you must decide whether to round up or round down.

Directions: Solve the following story problems.

1. Chandra is storing her family's sweaters in boxes for the summer. She has 18 sweaters. Each box will hold 4 sweaters.

   a. How many boxes does she need? 5 boxes

   b. What did you do with the remainder? Why?
   Round up. Add 1 box to hold the remaining sweaters.

2. The Library Club has $525 for a summer picnic.

   a. They use half of the money for food. How much money will they have left over for entertainment, decorations, and prizes? $262.50

   b. What did you do with the remainder? Why? The decimal form of the remainder is included in the answer. It becomes the cents.

3. The Library Club has $187 for prizes.

   a. How many $2 prizes could the club buy? 93 prizes

   b. How many $3 prizes could the club buy? 62 prizes

   c. What did you do with the remainder in each of these problems? Why? The remainder was disregarded. There will be some money left over, but not enough to buy another prize.

4. There are 152 people at the picnic. Six people can fit at each table.

   a. How many tables will be needed? 26 tables

   b. What did you do with the remainder? Why? Since there is a remainder, 1 more table must be added to make sure there is enough room for the remaining people.

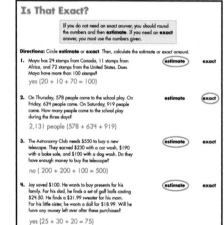

Expanding

Write a problem using division that has a remainder. Explain what the remainder means. How does the remainder affect the answer?

Answers will vary.

45

Multiple-Step Problems

Directions: Some problems take more than one step to solve. You must decide how to solve each step, and in which order to solve them.

1. Over summer break, Melissa and Emmitt worked at the movie theater. Melissa worked 6 hours each day, 3 days a week. Emmitt worked twice as many hours a week as Melissa. The season lasted 14 weeks. How many hours did each of them work during the season?

   a. How many hours did Melissa work each week? Show your work.
   18 hours per week (6 x 3)

   b. How many hours did Emmitt work each week? Show your work.
   36 hours per week (18 x 2)

   c. How many hours did Melissa work in the entire season? Show your work.
   252 hours (18 x 14)

   d. How many hours did Emmitt work for the entire season? Show your work.
   504 hours (36 x 14)

2. On a school trip, 3 buses of students go to the museum. Each bus has 54 students. Each student spends $7 on admission. How much money do the students spend altogether?

   a. How many students go to the museum? Show your work.
   162 students (3 x 54)

   b. How much money do the students spend altogether? Show your work.
   $1,134 ($7 x 162)

3. The Student Council is having a bake sale. The president brings 2 dozen sugar cookies. The vice president brings 3 dozen peanut-butter cookies. The secretary and treasurer each bring 60 chocolate-chip cookies. They are selling bags with 3 cookies each. How many bags of cookies do they have to sell? Show your work.

   60 bags (12 x 2 + 12 x 3 + 60 x 2 = 180; 180 ÷ 3 = 60)

Reflecting

Look at problem 1. Could you have solved the problem by answering the questions in a different order? Could you have used different steps to solve the problem? Explain.
Question a needs to be answered before any of the others. Questions b, c, and d could have been answered in a different order. Students could have found out how much Melissa made in a season and then doubled it to get Emmitt's amount.

46

Smart Shopper

Directions: Solve the following story problems.

1. Theo goes shopping for cereal. The same cereal is available in 2 different sizes. A 16 oz. box costs $4.37. A 20 oz. box costs $5.22. Which would be the best buy?

   a. If 16 oz. cost $4.37, 1 oz. would cost $4.37 ÷ 16 = __$0.27__.

   b. If 20 oz. cost $5.22, 1 oz. would cost __$5.22 ÷ 20__ = __$0.26__.

   c. The __20__ oz. box would be the better buy.

2. Kiwadin could buy a 3 lb. bag of oranges for $1.69. There are a dozen oranges in the bag. He could buy oranges separately for $0.20 each. Should he buy the oranges separately, or in a bag? Explain.

   Oranges in the bag cost $0.14 each ($1.69 ÷ 12 = 0.14), which is cheaper than buying them separately.

3. Charles bought a box of 50 baseball cards for $25.00. His friend Deshawn likes to buy cards in packs of 10 for $4.00 each. Which boy got the better buy? Explain.

   Deshawn ($0.40 per card, rather than $0.50 per card)

Explaining

How do you find the price per ounce if you know the price for 12 ounces?

Take the price for 12 oz. and divide by 12.

47

Is That Exact?

If you do not need an exact answer, you should round the numbers and then **estimate**. If you need an **exact** answer, you must use the numbers given.

Directions: Circle **estimate** or **exact**. Then, calculate the estimate or exact amount.

1. Maya has 24 stamps from Canada, 11 stamps from Africa, and 72 stamps from the United States. Does Maya have more than 100 stamps?   (estimate)   exact
   yes (20 + 10 + 70 = 100)

2. On Thursday, 578 people came to the school play. On Friday, 634 people came. On Saturday, 919 people came. How many people came to the school play during the three days?   estimate   (exact)
   2,131 people (578 + 634 + 919)

3. The Astronomy Club needs $550 to buy a new telescope. They earned $230 with a car wash, $190 with a bake sale, and $100 with a dog wash. Do they have enough money to buy the telescope?   (estimate)   exact
   no (200 + 200 + 100 = 500)

4. Jay saved $100. He wants to buy presents for his family. For his dad, he finds a set of golf balls costing $24.50. He finds a $31.99 sweater for his mom. For his little sister, he wants a doll for $18.99. Will he have any money left over after these purchases?   (estimate)   exact
   yes (25 + 30 + 20 = 75)

Explaining

For what type of questions is an estimate appropriate?
Estimates can be used to determine if there is greater than or less than a certain amount.

48

Use Your Head

Directions: Estimate and solve the problem in your head. Write your answer. Then, solve using paper and pencil. You may use any strategies you are comfortable using.

1. Danielle has 3 quarters in her pocket. She has 5 dimes in her backpack. She wants to buy a bag of chips and a pop for $1.09. Does she have enough money?
   .75
   + .50
   1.25   yes

2. Emily bought a package of 72 pencils with holiday toppers. She wants to give one to each person in her classroom, her brother's classroom, and her sister's classroom. She has 26 students in her class, her brother has 24 students in his class, and her sister has 25 students in her class. Does she have enough pencils for every person?
   26
   24
   + 25
   75   no

3. Miguel wants to purchase a binder for $3.52, a pack of pencils for 84¢, and 6 folders for 24¢ each. He has $5.00. Does he have enough money?
   $3.52
   .84
   + 1.44
   $5.80   no

4. Ramiro is collecting food package points. If he collects 475 points, he will have enough to order a computer game. He collected 57 in June, 107 in July, 230 in August, and 61 in September. Does he have enough to place his order?
   57
   107
   230
   + 61
   455   no

5. Maria needs enough donuts for two classrooms of 26. Donuts come in packages of 12. If she buys 4 packages, does she have enough or need to buy one more?
   26   12
   + 26   x 4
   52   48   buy one more

6. Brent needs 2,647 toothpicks to complete a sculpture. He has an open box with 847 toothpicks in it. He found a box at the store with 500 toothpicks in it. What is the smallest number of boxes he needs to complete his project?
   500
   500
   500
   + 500
   2,000
   + 847
   2,847   4 more

49

Money Riddles

Directions: Read the riddles to determine the coins. Then, show how you know your answers are correct.

1. All 8 of my coins are silver in color. Their total is 50¢. What are they?
   2 dimes and 6 nickels

2. I have 36¢. I have 1 each of 3 different coins. What are my coins?
   quarter, dime, and penny

3. I have 5 coins worth 86¢. None of the coins are nickels. What are the coins?
   3 quarters, 1 dime, and 1 penny

4. I have 2 different kinds of coins worth 52¢. There are 12 coins total. What are they?
   10 nickels and 2 pennies

5. I have 7 coins worth $1.10. I have no more than 3 of any coin. What are my coins?
   3 quarters, 3 dimes, 1 nickel

6. I have 5 coins worth 50¢. I have at least 2 different types of coins. What are the coins?
   1 quarter, 2 dimes, and 1 nickel

7. I have 74¢. I have 3 types of coins, but no nickels. I have an even number of each coin. What are the coins?
   2 quarters, 2 dimes, and 4 pennies

8. I have 2 types of coins. They equal 79¢. What are the coins?
   3 quarters and 4 pennies

Explaining

Show 2 ways to make 68¢. Choose one way and write a riddle for it.

Answers will vary.

50

Choose Your Operation

Directions: Read each problem. Circle the function you would use to solve it. Explain to a friend how you decided which operation to choose. Solve the problems.

+ ⊖ x ÷ 1. The red bike costs $154.78. The blue bike costs $132.50. How much more does the red bike cost?

+ − x ⊕ 2. The administration wants to assign 2,082 students to 6 schools. How many students are in each school?

+ − x ⊕ 3. 15,860 beads were put into 65 bags. How many beads are in each bag?

+ − ⊗ ÷ 4. Mike bought 4 new shirts. Each shirt cost $15.88. How much were the shirts before tax?

⊕ − x ÷ 5. There are 345 students at Valley Elementary and 409 students at Hilltop Elementary. How many students attend both schools?

+ − ⊗ ÷ 6. Jackie made a 74-minute long distance telephone call. Her mother charged her the 6¢ a minute from the phone bill. How much did Jackie owe her mother?

+ − ⊕ x 7. Tara reads 13 pages each night. How long does it take her to finish her 195-page book?

+ − ⊗ ÷ 8. The container holds enough mix to make 18 servings of mashed potatoes. If each serving needs 3 scoops of mix, how many scoops of mix are in the container?

+ ⊖ x ÷ 9. Matthew is required to practice his horn for 180 minutes a week. He has already practiced for 124 minutes. How many minutes does he still need to practice?

⊕ − x + 10. Jamal's family collects state quarters. They have 127 quarters in one container and 235 quarters in another container. How many quarters do they have altogether?

51

"Sum" Patterns

Directions: Find a pattern in each row of numbers. Continue the pattern. Describe the pattern.

1. 1, 2, 3, 5, 8, 13, __21__, __34__, __55__, __89__, __144__

2. 3, 5, 8, 13, 21, 34, __55__, __89__, __144__, __233__, __377__

3. 1, 4, 5, 9, 14, 23, __37__, __60__, __97__, __157__, __254__

4. 1, 3, 4, 7, 11, 18, __29__, __47__, __76__, __123__, __199__

5. 2, 4, 6, 10, 16, 26, __42__, __68__, __110__, __178__, __288__

Reflecting

What do each of these patterns have in common? Are they growing or decreasing patterns? How do they change? Why do you think this page is called "Sum" Patterns? These are all growing patterns. The next number is found by adding the two previous numbers. This page is call "Sum" Patterns because all the patterns involve finding sums.

52

Adding and Subtracting Patterns

If a pattern has a **steady rate**, it changes by the same amount each time.

Directions: Finish the number patterns. Describe each pattern.

1. 55 52 49 46 __43__ __40__ __37__ __34__
   subtract 3

2. 16 23 30 37 __44__ __51__ __58__ __65__
   add 7

3. 115 100 85 70 __55__ __40__ __25__ __10__
   subtract 15

4. 50 149 248 347 __446__ __545__ __644__ __743__
   add 99

5. Which of the patterns are **growing patterns**? How do you know?
   problems 2 and 4; numbers increase

6. Which of the patterns are **decreasing patterns**? How do you know?
   problems 1 and 3; numbers decrease

7. How does each of these patterns change?
   at a steady rate

Expanding

Write a pattern of your own. Describe your pattern. Compare your pattern with other patterns on this page. How is it the same? How is it different?

Answers will vary.

53

Number Patterns

Directions: Solve these number pattern problems.

1. Look at the number pattern.
   1 __+1__ 2 __+2__ 4 __+3__ 7 __+4__ 11 __+5__ 16 __+6__ 22

   a. Is this a **growing pattern** or a **decreasing pattern**? growing pattern

   b. Does this pattern change at a **steady rate**? no

   c. Write the amount of change below each pair of numbers. The first two pairs have been done for you.

   d. Describe the pattern from one number to the next. The amount of change increases by 1 each time.

2. Find the pattern. Fill in the missing numbers.
   52 43 35 28 22 __17__ __13__ __10__ __8__

   a. How is this pattern different from the pattern in problem 1?
   It is a decreasing pattern instead of a growing pattern.

   b. How is it similar to the pattern in problem 1?
   Neither grows at a steady rate.

   c. Describe the pattern from one number to the next.
   Subtract 1 less each time (-9, -8, -7, -6, -5, -4, -3, -2).

3. Look at the number pattern.
   33 __-8__ 25 __-6__ 19 __-4__ 15 __-2__ 13

   a. Is this a **growing pattern** or a **decreasing pattern**? decreasing pattern

   b. Write the amount of change below each pair of numbers. The first two pairs have been done for you. -8, -6, -4, -2

   c. Describe the pattern in the amount of change from one number to the next.
   Subtract 2 less each time.

54

Number Patterns (cont.)

Directions: Find the pattern. Fill in the missing numbers. Describe each pattern.

4. 78 67 58 51 __46__ __43__ __42__
   subtract 2 less each time

5. 4 7 13 22 34 __49__ __67__ __88__
   add 3 more each time

6. 7 9 13 19 __27__ __37__ __49__
   add 2 more each time

7. Write this growing pattern as a decreasing pattern. Describe the pattern.
   36   39   43   48   54   61
   61, 54, 48, 43, 39, 36; subtract 1 less each time

8. Write this decreasing pattern as a growing pattern. Describe the pattern.
   68   64   58   50   40   28
   28, 40, 50, 58, 64, 68; add 2 less each time

Comparing

Compare growing patterns and decreasing patterns. Explain how to examine a pattern to determine its type.

Answers will vary.

55

Let's Compare

Directions: Write > for greater than or < for less than.

1. 10,769 < 11,200   177,204 > 116,791   97,213 < 107,213

2. 86,190 > 84,993   981,203 > 918,203   72,218 < 75,003

3. 198,221 > 98,221   264,193 < 266,001   83,103 > 80,793

4. 656,183 < 665,183   199,820 > 198,993   55,186 > 54,939

5. Write the numbers in order on the chart below.

| 756,802 | 694,213 | 820,000 | 971,246 | 378,461 | 192,874 |
| 471,622 | 216,606 | 92,813 | 87,214 | 63,744 | 55,806 |

	Big		Bigger		Biggest
1.	55,806	5.	192,874	9.	694,213
2.	63,744	6.	216,606	10.	756,802
3.	87,214	7.	378,461	11.	820,000
4.	92,813	8.	471,622	12.	971,246

6. The smallest number is __55,806__
   The largest number is __971,246__

7. Write the number that is 10 less than the smallest number. __55,796__
   Write the number that is 100 more than the smallest number. __55,906__
   Write the number that is 1,000 more than the largest number. __972,246__

56

You're the Greatest!

Directions: Compare each pair of numbers. Write < or > in each ◯.

1. 5,361 > 5,300
2. 9,327 > 9,237
3. 10,561 < 10,651
4. 593,461 < 593,614
5. 98,997 < 100,016
6. 497,843 > 496,912
7. 600,000 < 600,010
8. 1,493,017 < 1,947,413
9. 31,113,311 > 13,331,113
10. 1,087,789 > 987,911
11. 235,400 > 234,900
12. 893,982 > 892,983
13. 203,960 < 230,141
14. 156,651 < 651,156
15. 93,825 < 94,053
16. 23,985,310 < 29,385,013
17. 19,675,902 < 20,001,000
18. 63,814,910 > 59,950,418

Directions: Arrange the numbers in each group from the least to the greatest.

1. 59,359; 590,359; 509,359; 95,359
   59,359; 95,359; 509,359; 590,359

2. 417,003; 950,398; 409,985; 398,051
   398,051; 409,985; 417,003; 950,398

3. 24,890; 20,561; 24,279; 24,385
   20,561; 24,279; 24,385; 24,890

4. 831,485; 813,485; 89,497; 830,549
   89,497; 813,485; 830,549; 831,485

57

On the Average . . .

An **average** is found by adding numbers and dividing them by the total number of addends. See the example in the box.

The children on the 6-on-6 basketball team made the following number of baskets:

April	1	Beth	3
Colton	3	Ryan	1
Jen	2	J.J.	2

The school paper wants to write about the game, but they don't have room for such a long list. Instead, the reporter will find the **average** by following the steps below.

Steps

1. **Add** all the team members' baskets together.
   __1__ + __3__ + __2__ + __3__ + __1__ + __2__ = __12__

2. **Count** to find out how many team members there were.
   __6__

3. **Divide** your answer for step 1 by the number in step 2.
   __12__ ÷ __6__ = __2__

The paper will report that each team member normally makes an average of 2 baskets each. **Remember:** add, count, divide.

Directions: Find the average for the following problem:
In their last 3 games, the Longlegs scored 24 points, 16 points, and 20 points.

1. Add   2. Count   3. Divide. __20__
   24 + 16 + 20 = 60   3   3)60
                                    -6
What was their average? 20 points each game   00

58

Odd and Even Tug of War

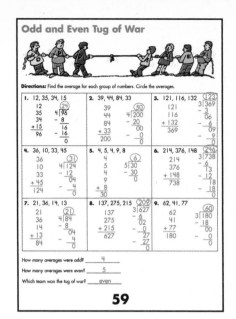

Directions: Find the average for each group of numbers. Circle the averages.

1. 12, 35, 34, 15
12
35   (24)
34   4⟌96
+15   − 8
96   16
− 16
0

2. 39, 44, 84, 33
39
44   (50)
84   4⟌200
+33   − 20
200   00
− 0
0

3. 121, 116, 132
121   (123)
116   3⟌369
+132 − 3
369   06
− 6
09
− 9
0

4. 36, 10, 33, 45
36
10   (31)
33   4⟌124
+45   − 12
124   04
− 4
0

5. 4, 5, 4, 9, 8
4
5   (6)
4   5⟌30
9   − 30
+8   0
30

6. 214, 376, 148
214   (246)
376   3⟌738
+148 − 6
738   13
− 12
18
− 18
0

7. 21, 36, 14, 13
21
36   (21)
14   4⟌84
+13   − 8
84   04
− 4
0

8. 137, 275, 215
137   (209)
275   3⟌627
+215 − 6
627   02
− 0
27
− 27
0

9. 62, 41, 77
62   (60)
41   3⟌180
+77   − 18
180   00
− 0
0

How many averages were odd? ___4___
How many averages were even? ___5___
Which team won the tug of war? ___even___

59

Find the Lucky Number

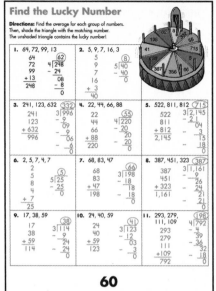

Directions: Find the average for each group of numbers. Then, shade the triangle with the matching number. The unshaded triangle contains the lucky number!

1. 64, 72, 99, 13
64   (62)
72   4⟌248
99   − 24
+13   08
248   − 8
0

2. 5, 9, 7, 16, 3
5   (8)
9   5⟌40
7   − 40
16   0
+ 3
40

3. 241, 123, 632
241   (332)
123   3⟌996
+632 − 9
996   09
− 9
06
− 6
0

4. 22, 44, 66, 88
22   (55)
44   4⟌220
66   − 20
+88   20
220   − 20
0

5. 522, 811, 812
522   (715)
811   3⟌2,145
+812 − 21
2,145 04
− 3
15
− 15
0

6. 2, 5, 7, 4, 7
2   (5)
5   5⟌25
7   − 25
4   0
+ 7
25

7. 68, 83, 47
68   (66)
83   3⟌198
+47   − 18
198   18
− 18
0

8. 387, 451, 323
387   (387)
451   3⟌1,161
+323 − 9
1,161 26
− 24
21
− 21
0

9. 17, 38, 59
17   (38)
38   3⟌114
+59   − 9
114   24
− 24
0

10. 24, 40, 59
24   (41)
40   3⟌123
+59   − 12
123   03
− 3
0

11. 293, 279, 111, 109
293   (198)
279   4⟌792
111   − 4
+109 39
792   − 36
32
− 32
0

60

Divide It Up

Directions: Divide. Write the letter of each problem above its answer below.

I. 34⟌2584 = 76   **I.** 42⟌8526 = 203   **O.** 63⟌6237 = 99   **D.** 55⟌3575 = 65

D. 89⟌6319 = 71   **Y.** 90⟌1800 = 20   **T.** 31⟌6231 = 201   **U.** 18⟌882 = 49

Y O U   D I D   I T !
20 99 49   65 203 71   76 201

Directions: Find the total test scores below. Then, find the averages.

Students	Test Scores					Total	Average
Sue Ann	18	20	17	19	16	90	18
James	15	14	17	16	13	75	15
Tommy	19	19	20	18	19	95	19
Carlos	16	19	18	17	16	86	17.2
Anna	20	20	19	20	19	98	19.6

Who has the highest average? ___Anna___
Who needs to study more? ___James___

61

Better Than the Average Team

5 to 3
PLAY
SCORE RUN
Bears-48
Rams-59
Eagles-70
Rams-40
Run
36 to 17
Cougars-52
Wolverines-68

The sports editor o our local news a er needs our el averaging te team scores a ter te irst ive games o te season

Directions: olve to ind te scoring average o eac team

Team	Points					Average
Bears	63	58	64	59	61	61 ts
Falcons	48	46	62	54	50	52 ts
Rams	49	54	46	57	49	51 ts
Eagles	70	71	67	62	65	67 ts
Red Hawks	65	68	60	61	61	63 ts
Cougars	62	56	57	68	52	59 ts
Wolverines	58	63	55	56	68	60 ts
Wildcats	52	56	54	49	54	53 ts

62

It All Averages Out!

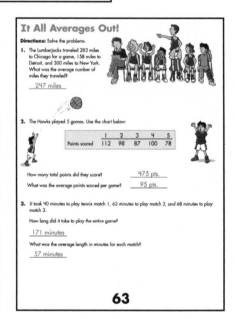

Directions: Solve the problems.

1. The Lumberjacks traveled 283 miles to Chicago for a game, 158 miles to Detroit, and 300 miles to New York. What was the average number of miles they traveled?

___247 miles___

2. The Hawks played 5 games. Use the chart below:

	1	2	3	4	5
Points scored	112	98	87	100	78

How many total points did they score? ___475 pts.___
What was the average points scored per game? ___95 pts.___

3. It took 40 minutes to play tennis match 1, 63 minutes to play match 2, and 68 minutes to play match 3.

How long did it take to play the entire game?

___171 minutes___

What was the average length in minutes for each match?

___57 minutes___

63

Keeping Track

Rob is training for the javelin throw at a big track meet. He wants to know how he is doing, so he records the distances of 10 throws he makes during practice.

Directions: Find Rob's average distance.
___22.9 feet or 23 feet___

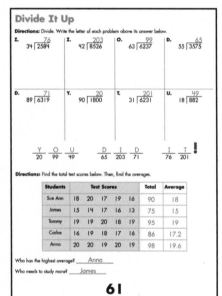

Throw	Distance	Throw	Distance
1	23 feet	6	20 feet
2	26 feet	7	24 feet
3	21 feet	8	23 feet
4	23 feet	9	22 feet
5	25 feet	10	22 feet

The average of a group of numbers tells something about the main trend of the data. The three most important kinds of averages are called the **mode**, the **median**, and the **mean**.

MODE
The number that occurs most often

The **mode** is the number in the data that occurs most often. The mode of the javelin distances is 23 feet, since that number appears three times—more than any other does.

If the data do not have a number that appears more than once, there is no mode. For example, the numbers 6, 4, 8, 7, 5, 3, and 9 have no mode.

A group of numbers can also have more than one mode. For example, the numbers 2, 5, 4, 3, 2, 3, and 6 have two modes since 2 and 3 both occur twice.

If a group of numbers does have a mode, the mode will always be one of the numbers in the list.

64

Keeping Track Again

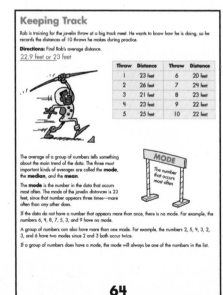

Directions: Find the mode.

3, 6, 9, 5, 12, 5, 7, 8 ___5___

11, 7, 9, 11, 3, 8, 9, 10, 11 ___11___

8, 5, 6, 4, 7, 11, 10, 9 ___none___   5, 7, −2, 4, −5, −2, 0, 2, 1 ___−2___

4, 7, 5, 6, 7, 4, 3, 4, 8, 4, 7, 7 ___7, 4___   3, 4, 3, 2, 0, 0, 1, 2, 0, 1 ___0___

3, 3, 3, 3, 3, 3, 3, 3, 3, 3 ___3___   1, 2, 3, 4, 5, 6, 7, 8, 9 ___none___

1, 2, 3, 1, 2, 3, 1, 2, 3, 1, 2, 3 ___1, 2, 3___   13, 12, 10, 15, 12, 14, 12, 11 ___12___

Directions: Solve the problems.

1. All of Jill's throws landed 24 feet away. What is the mode? ___24 feet___

2. On page 21, look at Rob's data for his first ten throws. How far would he have to throw the javelin on the 11th throw so that the data would have two modes? ___22 feet___

3. Write a list of 6 numbers that have no mode. ___Answers will vary.___

4. Which javelin thrower below had a higher mode? ___Kate___

Kate	Adam
22 feet	21 feet
23	20
24	23
24	24
21	21
22	22
22	25

65

78

Advanced Concepts: Grade 4

Jumping the Median

The **median** is another kind of average. When ordering a list of numbers from least to greatest, the median is the number that falls in the middle. Look at Anna's maximum high jumps for the last week.

Day	Height
Monday	62 inches
Tuesday	64 inches
Wednesday	62 inches
Thursday	64 inches
Friday	60 inches
Saturday	61 inches
Sunday	64 inches

Order the numbers: 60, 61, 62, **62**, 64, 64, 64. The number **62** falls in the middle. It is the median.

The mode is 64 inches. In some cases, the median and mode are the same number.

MEDIAN
The middle number in an ordered list of numbers

If there is an even number of heights, there will be two numbers in the middle. To find the median, add the two middle numbers and divide the sum by 2.

Example: 2, 2, 3, 4, 6, 6, 7, 9

The numbers **4** and **6** are both in the middle. 4 + 6 = 10; 10 ÷ 2 = 5. The median is **5**. The median does not have to be a number in the list.

Directions: Find the median.

3, 6, 9, 5, 12, 5, 8 ___6___   11, 7, 9, 11, 3, 8, 9, 10 ___9___

11, 6, 4, 7, 5, 9, 11, 10 ___8___   -4, 2, -3, -1, 1, -1, -2 ___-1___

7, 5, 6, 4, 7, 11, 10, 9 ___7___   2, 4, 6, 8, 10, 12, 14, 16 ___9___

3, 3, 3, 3, 3, 3, 3, 3, 3 ___3___   0, 1, 4, -2, 3, -1, -2 ___0___

55, 34, 67, 39, 47, 18, 46, 55, 61 ___47___   2, -2, 1, -1, 3, -4 ___0___

66

What Do You Mean?

Probably the most common average is the **mean**. To find the mean, add all the numbers in the list. Then, divide the sum by the total number of addends.

Suppose a hurdler completes his trials in the following times. Find the mean.

Trial	Time in Seconds
1	35
2	29
3	34
4	30
5	31
6	33

MEAN
The sum of all the numbers divided by the number of addends

Add the numbers: 35 + 29 + 34 + 30 + 31 + 33 = 192
Divide 192 by 6 because there are 6 numbers in the list: 192 ÷ 6 = 32.
The mean is 32 seconds.

The mean may or may not be a number in the list. The mean may also be different from the median and/or the mode.

Directions: Find the mean.

3, 6, 9, 5, 12 ___7___   11, 5, 9, 11, 3, 7, 9, 9 ___8___

3, 1, 0, 2, 0, 0 ___1___   4, 6, -1, -1 ___2___

-3, -2, -3, -1, -1 ___-2___   2, -1, 1, -2 ___0___

3, 3, 3, 3, 3, 3, 3, 3, 3, 3 ___3___   5, 9, 6, 2, 7, 9, 12, 4, 8, 8 ___7___

9, 4, 5, 2, 6, 0, 3, 4, 3 ___4___   6, 7, 3, 6, 4, 2, 7, 5 ___5___

67

What Do You Mean by Median?

The **mean** is the average found by adding all values and dividing by the number of values. The **median** is the number that is exactly in the middle of the data.

Example: Lenny loves basketball. He scored the following points per game.

Game	Points
#1	5
#2	10
#3	3
#4	14
#5	3

Median: 3, 3, ⑤, 10, 14
The median is 5 points per game.

Mean: 5 + 10 + 3 + 14 + 3 = 35
35 ÷ 5 = 7
The mean is an average of 7 points per game.

Directions: Study the data to correctly answer the questions.

Student	No. of Books Read
Anna	9
Carlos	5
Brian	7
Jada	8
Lin	11

1. List the numbers you would add and what you would divide them by to determine the mean number of books read by each student.

   (9 + 5 + 7 + 8 + 11) ÷ 5 = mean

2. What is the mean? ___8___

3. What is the median? ___8___

Tanya's scout troop made beaded animals to sell and raise funds for a camping trip.

Troop Members	No. of Bead Animals Made
Tanya	17
Cho	15
Maria	11
Avishai	14
Lucy	9
Kaly	6
Yong	21
Maya	6
Beth	9

4. List the numbers you would add and what you would divide them by to determine the mean number of beaded animals made by each troop member.

   (17 + 15 + 11 + 14 + 9 + 6 + 21 + 6 + 9) ÷ 9 = mean

5. What is the mean? ___12___

6. What is the median? ___11___

68

Finding Mean

Directions: Read the passage and answer the questions.

What is the average number of people who walk by your house between 3:00 P.M. and 4:00 P.M. during the week? Are you interested in finding out the answer to this question? You'll need to find the **mean**, or average of the data. If you record that 25 people pass by on Monday, 32 people pass by on Tuesday, 34 people pass by on Wednesday, 18 people pass by on Thursday, and 31 people pass by on Friday, you have gathered the information you need. To answer the question, you will need to find the average of all five numbers. Start by finding the sum of all five numbers. Then, divide the sum by 5 to find the average number of people who walk by your house each day between 3:00 P.M. and 4:00 P.M. Based on the information gathered above, the average number of people who walk by is 28.

1. Write a definition for the word **mean**.

   The mean is the average.

2. What should you do after you find the sum of all five numbers?

   After you find the sum of all five numbers, you should divide by 5.

3. What would you need to do first if you wanted to find the average number of people who walked by your house between 9:00 A.M. and 10:00 A.M.?

   First, you would need to count the number of people who pass by your house between 9:00 and 10:00 a.m. for several days.

4. What does "28" answer in the article above?

   the average number of people that walked by between 3:00 and 4:00 P.M.

5. Find the mean of the following five numbers: 65, 34, 76, 54, and 66.

   59

69

Notes